Fashion and Design

Ken Baynes is a design consultant and writer. He trained as a painter and stained-glass designer at the Royal College of Art and became interested in mass media and popular education. In the late 1960s he worked with the Welsh Arts Council to pioneer a series of exhibitions about Art and Society and has also organized and designed exhibitions for the National Portrait Gallery and the Science Museum in London and in Australia, Sweden and the United States.

For four years he was head of the Design Education Unit at the Royal College of Art. He is now education consultant to the government-funded Design Dimension project and the Royal Fine Art Commission. He has also published many popularizing and technical books and worked on two television series about design.

Krysia Brochocka is a ceramicist and pioneer in the field of design education. She was trained as a primary-school teacher and then worked at the Roehampton Institute of Higher Education, where she first ran the ceramics department at Digby Stuart College. She then took an MA in design education at the Royal College of Art. She has been educational materials consultant to Marshall Cavendish, developed the textiles section of the *Young Blood* exhibition and worked with Ken Baynes and Beverly Saunders on *Automated Nostalgia*, a show of work by young British graphic and fashion designers that took Minneapolis by storm in 1985.

Krysia Brochocka is now a member of the government's National Curriculum Working Party for design and technology.

Beverly Saunders is an illustrator and writer who, since graduating from the Royal School of Art in 1985, has specialized in devising educational materials for children. In 1983 she won the British Museum Design Award of the Royal Society of Arts and in 1985 brought out the first titles in a new series of children's materials for the National Trust. In the same year she joined Ken Baynes and Krysia Brochocka to organize *Automated Nostalgia* and since then has extended her work to include a series of storybooks for children (yet to be published) and a wide range of illustration and surface-pattern work.

She has taught regularly at Nottingham Polytechnic and is now an external examiner for the CNAA at Manchester Polytechnic.

Fashion and Design

Ken Baynes,
Krysia Brochocka and
Beverly Saunders

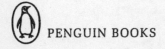 PENGUIN BOOKS

PENGUIN BOOKS

Published by the Penguin Group
27 Wrights Lane, London W8 5TZ, England
Viking Penguin Inc., 40 West 23rd Street, New York, New York 10010, USA
Penguin Books Australia Ltd, Ringwood, Victoria, Australia
Penguin Books Canada Ltd, 2801 John Street, Markham, Ontario, Canada L3R 1B4
Penguin Books (NZ) Ltd, 182–190 Wairau Road, Auckland 10, New Zealand

Penguin Books Ltd, Registered Offices: Harmondsworth, Middlesex, England

First published 1990

10 9 8 7 6 5 4 3 2 1

Filmset in Linotron 202 Melior

Typeset, printed and bound in Great Britain by
BPCC Hazell Books
Aylesbury, Bucks, England
Member of BPCC Ltd.

Contents

Contents

Acknowledgements

This book could not have been produced without the wholehearted support and enthusiasm of the people and organizations who are presented in the case studies. We are tremendously grateful to them for their time, trouble and patience.

Special thanks to the Nottingham Fashion Workshops who allowed us to use their excellent information service and gave much helpful advice. And to Di Eagle, our assistant, who typed and retyped the manuscript through its successive versions!

Ken Baynes
Krysia Brochocka
Beverly Saunders

Oakham, April 1989

Introduction

Many people are attracted by the idea of working in fashion design. It sounds glamorous. Fashion has a high profile. It is often in the news. Famous designers appear to lead exotic lives, jetting around the world to get inspiration and sell their expensive products.

One aim of this Self-Starter is to dispel that image. Fashion is an important, fascinating and often rewarding industry to work in but it takes place in back street studios, huge old mills and bright new chain stores more often than on the beach of Acapulco or the catwalk of the London Fashion Show.

Looked at more realistically, fashion is a huge and complex international industry made up of companies and groups that range in size from Marks and Spencer, employing 70,000 people, to individual designer-makers who work on their own with only the dog for company.

The fashion industry is extraordinarily diverse, not only in scale of operations, but in the way it is organized and the roles people play. It includes wholesaling and retailing as well as manufacturing, but some knowledge of design is important throughout the industry. Why is this? Because the whole industry depends on creating products that people want to buy. Getting these products right is the only way to succeed in the fashion business. Designers have the specific job of designing products but actually developing them is the result of team work. Sales people, representatives, buyers, pattern cutters and managers all need to be aware of the tastes, ideas, possibilities and constraints that will ensure the success of what is made. They need to know about design.

Fashion is not just designing and making clothes. It is an industry with well-developed supporting journalism, advertising and media coverage. It has to create the right atmosphere and image in the style and layout of its shops. It relies on designers with an understanding of fashion to create photographs, videos, advertisements and magazines and to plan interiors and corporate identity programmes.

Against this background of diversity, it is impossible to identify the 'best' route into fashion design. There are many effective routes.

To some extent where you begin will, however, determine where you end up. Get a degree in business management and you are more likely to be the manager of a product range than to do the detailed design work on garments. Start on the factory floor and your knowledge of the practicalities of production will always be valued. Learn the art of pattern grading and you will be in demand when clothes are being detailed for mass production. Start in a shop and your influence as a buyer could help determine the style and feel, the design, of whole ranges of clothes.

Good courses in fashion design exist in Britain. Their graduates have an enviable international reputation for flair and inventiveness but more everyday qualities are also encouraged on some courses. Young British designers are in demand. Courses that combine technological study with design ability are surprisingly rare. Courses are available at HNC, HND, degree and postgraduate level. It is hard to select the right course. Here again, where you want to end up is an important consideration when choosing where to begin.

This Self-Starter sets out to give you a useful picture of the fashion industry and the role of design within it. Much of the information is presented in the form of up-to-date (1989) case studies of selected organizations and interviews with people working on the design side of the industry. These give a good impression of the variety of opportunities that exist and the career patterns of people who have made use of them.

Part 1   The World of Fashion Design

The first part of this book introduces some basic facts and ideas about fashion design and the fashion industry. It then focuses down to identify the role of designers in creating the clothes and accessories we buy and wear. It traces the way in which garments are designed, developed, made and marketed and gives a list of the jobs that are involved in the process.

1 What is Fashion?

The fashion industry has a deceptive public face. What gets into the newspapers and on to television is all about a very particular fragment of the whole. The clothes worn by the rich and famous and the collections produced by well-known designers are important. They are a source of vitality but they certainly are not typical. In terms of the industry as an industry it is, of course, mass production and high street shops that are typical. It is here that the economic foundation of clothing and textiles is to be found. As the tills ring up the sales on a Saturday morning in Surbiton or Cumbernauld, Gateshead or Plymouth, they ring up continuing work for managers, designers, salespeople, cutters, machinists, weavers, fashion journalists, van drivers, photographers, cleaners and tea ladies. In the end, it is the mass of ordinary consumers who decide the future of the fashion industry. The acid test is in millions and millions of individual sales and the satisfaction – or disappointment – that they give.

With the exception of food and drink, there can be no other industry that has such an intimate interaction with the lives and tastes of its customers. How people look is a reflection of their personality and their role. Am I a conformist? I can signal the information to you easily by what I wear. You can learn important things about me long before I open my mouth. Am I off to a party, going to the office, on the way to dig a ditch or drive a train? Clothes are functional but they also communicate in a language that everyone uses and understands.

Human beings seem always to have needed to use clothes in three fundamentally different ways:

1 *Utilitarian*   Here the need is to keep out cold or heat, to give protection against the weather, to provide comfort and security indoors and out. At the most extreme, in mining or space research, for example, protective clothes and related equipment are essential to the job. The same can apply in sport. Babies and handicapped or

ill people may need clothes which compensate for their inability to do things for themselves.

2 *Psychological*   Here the need is to express one's own personality in dress. Clothes say: 'This is me, this is my character, this is my attitude to life.' It is not only extravagant dress that works in this way; a sober business suit is saying 'this is me' just as much as clothes that seem outrageous or individualistic.

3 *Social*   Here the need is to communicate membership, belief, rank or status. The idea does not apply only to uniforms. Young people dress in a particular way to express their group identity with the young just as, on Remembrance Sunday, the veteran soldiers are identified by the solemn formality of their civilian clothes. The social uses of dress are very elaborate, ranging from communicating sexual status and occupation to conformity with the notions of 'good taste' held by a particular social class.

In all wealthy societies, the majority of clothes set out to serve all three areas of need, often at the same time. We want our clothes to be reasonably practical but they have to satisfy our personal taste while also being socially acceptable in the group to which we belong.

The word 'wealthy' is important. The growth of fashion, as opposed simply to the supply of clothing, depends on there being resources to spare for the elaboration of clothes above and beyond what is utilitarian. In order to be able to use clothes to express feelings, ideas and status, people must have sufficient disposable wealth to pay for the extra time, materials and workmanship that this entails. There is an interesting parallel with building. Basic, humble buildings can be very satisfying but it is only with greater resources that architecture can express the particular spirit of an age, the philosophical and aesthetic ideas of its time.

It may be objected that clothes are on a different level to architecture. Fashion is often thought of as superficial. But, in their own way, clothes capture the ideas and fantasies of people even more effectively than buildings because they are more intimate and more personal. It is hard not to imagine Tudor buildings filled with Elizabethan ladies and gentlemen in their elaborate and confident clothes, or Victorian factories presided over by frock-coated, top-hatted manufacturers directing what was then the workshop of the world. Like all consciously made things, fashionable clothes change over time, telling the story of the people who designed them, bought them and delighted in them. Fashion is an essential part of our picture of the past.

What has happened during the last fifty years in industrialized societies is that changing fashions have ceased to be the prerogative of the wealthy few and become something the majority of people can share. Behind this development stand technology and mass production. So long as handwork was the normal way of making things, elaboration remained expensive. However ill paid the workers there was a bottom limit to the cost of a fashionable garment. Although textile manufacture was mechanized at the start of the industrial revolution and sewing machines came into use in the 1860s, small armies of seamstresses and tailors laboured away in sweat shops well into the twentieth century.

Reduction in cost is only half the story. Industrialization also created wealth and eventually encouraged its spread throughout society. Disposable wealth finally came to millions of working- and lower-middle-class people with the first prosperous years of the 1950s. The effect on the fashion industry was dramatic: it opened the door to an explosion of change and experiment. Mass production and widespread affluence pulled mass clothing kicking and screaming into the fashion world of the twentieth century. Fed by young people with spending power, the consumer boom began in earnest.

What happened in Britain in the 1950s was not an isolated event. The whole of the industrialized world took part. A vast, international market emerged and with it some very significant changes of direction. Up to 1939, Paris and the taste of the established middle class dominated the content of fashion design. Dior's New Look of the immediate post-war years was the final fling of this exclusive grip on style. Immediately afterwards, the United States established its leadership by providing a universal design language for teenagers, and this was quickly followed by Britain where the miniskirt and the Mini car became international symbols of the Swinging Sixties.

The direction of flow that used to be exclusively from the top down has been broken and redirected into many new channels.

Teddy Boys, Mods and Rockers, Punks and New Romantics are all recent influential styles with their roots on the street. The motive power came from 'below'. The visual resources of history, pop music, advertising and the media are now ransacked to find exactly the right answer to fashion's essential problem: what comes next? What are people going to buy next?

The fashion industry is frequently criticized for dictating to people. It is said that customers will buy what they are told to buy, that they do not have a real choice because, in any one year, the clothes in the shops are really all the same. What it offers is not individuality but conformity with the style of the moment. There obviously is some truth in this. It is a part of the meaning of fashion that it changes in a self-consistent way. If it did not, it would be impossible to distinguish the fashionable clothes of the 1790s from the fashionable clothes of the 1890s or the 1990s. Fashion always offers individuality within a prevailing style. But what that prevailing style will be cannot, in today's conditions, simply be decided on by designers and manufacturers. Even the formidable power of marketing, advertising and the media cannot persuade people to buy and wear clothes that do not capture the way they feel about themselves and the times they live in.

Effective fashion – fashion that sells and sets its seal on a particular moment – is created by designers who can understand these popular undercurrents of taste and feeling. What they have to do then is to give form to the intangible. They have to convert ideas and emotions into the physical reality of cloth and cut. It used to be thought that the ability to do this depended on genius and insight. No doubt all really superlative design work in any field depends to some degree on intuition but the emphasis today is on professionalism. What is needed is sufficient reliability to make consistently accurate predictions about what will or will not sell.

Mary Troxell and Elaine Stone, joint authors of the American standard work on fashion merchandising,* go so far as to describe this predictive work as a 'science of fashion'. Science does not seem to be quite the right word for it. Fashion does not obey anything like the physical laws of nature. On the other hand, it certainly is possible

* *Fashion Merchandising*, Mary D. Troxell and Elaine Stone, McGraw-Hill, New York 1981.

to identify and understand the principles and influences that make it what it is. Anyone wishing to enter fashion design will need to know something about these fundamentals. You will be wise to study them in greater depth by going to shows and exhibitions and by further reading but it is useful to introduce them here.

Fashion is Dynamic

Change and competition are the lifeblood of fashion. Social upheavals, changes in taste, wars, new ideas in art: these are just some of the external influences which shape fashion. Within the industry itself the influence of great retail houses, individual designers, new technology, marketing skill and finance interact to decide who is taking the edge at any one particular moment. Fashion is itself the subject of fashion – it is a volatile world in which a sudden craze may make a manufacturer's fortune and where the creative centre of gravity can shift unpredictably from London to New York to Paris to Milan and suddenly back to London again via Tokyo.

Fashion is Cyclical

All historians of design have noticed that fashion moves like the swing of a pendulum. James Laver* points out how the focus of sexual attention moves around the body and that fashionable clothes follow it at a discreet distance! Agnes Brooke Young† believes that only three basic silhouettes have ever been used for fashionable women's clothes. She says that fashion moves on systematically from one shape to the next. Since the Second World War, skirt lengths have moved up and down, each change leading into the next. There is an internal logic to these cyclical changes that designers are in tune with and which they respond to and shape by their own work.

The cyclical nature of fashion is important commercially. Manufacturers and retailers use the term 'fashion cycle' to describe the way in which a particular style grows in popularity and eventually declines. It is usually seen as having five stages:

* *Taste and Fashion*, James Laver, Harrap and Co., New York 1946 (revised).
† *Recurring Cycles of Fashion, 1760–1937*, Agnes Brooke Young, Harper and Bros, New York 1937.

> Introduction
> Rise
> Culmination
> Decline
> Obsolescence

James Laver explained the phenomenon another way. Every style, he said, goes through a sequence in which it gradually gains acceptance and then gradually loses it. Worn ten years before its time it might cause outrage, be called 'indecent' and cause dismay and condemnation. Then things would change:

> 'Shameless' five years before its time
> 'Outré' one year before its time
> 'Smart' in its time
> 'Dowdy' one year after its time
> 'Hideous' ten years after its time
> 'Ridiculous' twenty years after its time

This cycle would be faster today and we might use different words but the rise and fall of styles remains a fact of life in the fashion industry. Each stage in the cycle offers commercial possibilities and different sectors of the industry are geared to meeting them, even down to second-hand clothes that were once shameless, then smart, then ridiculous and have now become outré and interesting for a second time.

Troxell and Stone quote Paul Poiret, a great designer in the 1920s who said that all fashion cycles end in 'excess' and they cite the miniskirt that became so brief as to be practically non-existent and the huge hoop skirt of the eighteenth century that ended up eight feet wide. 'Once the extreme in styling has been reached, a fashion is nearing its end. The attraction of the fashion wanes and people begin to seek a different look – a new fashion.'

Economic Conditions Influence Fashion

We have already seen that economic growth and mass production created the modern fashion industry. But the influence of economic factors can also be more finely detailed and identified. In his book

On Human Finery,* Quentin Bell showed that the abandonment of traditional peasant costumes was directly related to the growth of industrialization. Other observers see a definite link between skirt lengths and prosperity – skirts are long in a slump and rise when the stock-markets rise. The idea may seem far-fetched at first but there is no doubt that people's moods are deeply affected by the general economic circumstances and find expression in what they buy and wear.

In a broader sense, fashion is one of the areas that reacts quickly to change in the economy. This is easy to understand. In hard times, it is possible to postpone buying a new coat for several years before sheer necessity takes over. Many fashion purchases are optional. Fashion therefore depends not only on the general health of the economy but on a specific aspect of it – the growth of disposable personal incomes and the proportion of incomes available for optional spending. Put crudely, whatever group has the larger disposable income available for optional spending will dominate the fashion scene. Designers and manufacturers will set out to meet their needs. Teenagers with money to spend created the dominant fashion of the 1950s, just as young middle-class professionals – yuppies – do today.

It follows that designers must be aware of demographic changes and their effect on markets. In Britain, the age structure of the population is changing dramatically. The proportion of young people is falling and the proportion of elderly people is growing. At the same time, old people are leading more varied and active lives. What kinds of clothes will these people want to buy and how much money will they have available? Getting the answer right is an important puzzle for the fashion industry.

Social Changes Influence Fashion

Because it serves people so intimately, fashion responds to social change with great rapidity. The journey made by fashion from the stiff, formal clothes of the Edwardian age to the loose, informal clothes of the 1980s holds up a mirror to the wider changes in British

* *On Human Finery*, Quentin Bell, The Hogarth Press, London 1947.

social life. It is not only women's clothes that have been transformed. Look at any photograph of a seaside promenade before 1914: it will be crowded with men dressed in suits and jackets and every single one of them will be wearing a hat!

As we have already pointed out, the most important single social change since 1900 has been the admittance of working- and lower-middle-class people to the world of fashion. Their huge buying power made it certain that their tastes and attitudes would influence fashion style from 1950 onwards. The effect has been paradoxical. A breath of outrageous fresh air roared through the fifties and sixties but this seems to have run out of steam and inspiration with the demise of punk. Now the emphasis in the mass market is more middle of the road, reflecting perhaps the expansion of the middle class, the wide acceptance of middle-class values and the movement of once-young rebels into middle-aged domesticity.

What other social changes have been important?

Wars   There seems no doubt that the two World Wars pushed forward social and psychological changes. They called old values into question and encouraged a desire for revolutionary change. They fuelled the desire for a more equal world. Each war was followed by a period of exuberance in fashion design and this period of daring stamped itself on everything that followed. The general influence of wars on fashion has been to destroy formality and to pave the way for innovation.

New roles for women   The suffragettes looked for emancipation wearing clothes that vividly symbolized their subservience and lack of freedom. In the First World War, women found themselves doing men's jobs and, in its aftermath, refused to return to restrictive Edwardian clothes. The war brought about the deaths of millions of young men and this in turn meant that, for the first time, many single women pursued an independent career. They demanded suitable work clothes from fashion designers. The Second World War repeated and enormously strengthened the social effects of the First and saw the beginnings of a new and coherent women's movement. But at the same time, the wars had a revolutionary effect on sexual customs which in turn completely transformed and magnified the overtly sexual content of clothes.

So here again there is a paradox. As a result of women playing new roles, the diversity of their clothes has grown and, above all, become more practical. But the sexual significance of women's clothes has remained strong in a way that some people find incompatible with real independence and individuality. For designers, and the women they serve, the most dramatic result has been to widen enormously the range of meanings conveyed by women's clothes. The subtle transformations wrought by social and economic change are equally subtly captured and communicated by the symbolic and cultural references to be found in fashion. Women can 'say' more things through clothes than they have ever been able to say before.

Sport and entertainment As the twentieth century moved on, sport and entertainment became more and more important in people's lives. They devoted time to leisure and identified sport with health. Sport, in particular, has influenced everyday dress, leading the race towards informality and 'looseness'. The growth of leisure has blurred the distinction between what to wear for work and what to wear for play.

The worlds of fashion and entertainment have always been closely linked. Paris *couturiers* at the turn of the century would often 'adopt' an actress or singer, dressing her exclusively in an exaggerated version of their normal range to act as a living advertisement for their skills. Since the 1950s, pop music, film and television have become accepted as major sources of fashion ideas. The Beatles brought widely flared trousers and frilly shirts to a short season of prominence while Woody Allen's film *Annie Hall* seems to have influenced the fashion consciousness of the whole of the 1970s. It would be easy to extend the list. In the future fashion will contrive to respond to social changes and it will be the designer's job to anticipate those changes and embody them in products. Two conundrums for the future might be: how will the 'green' consciousness about the environment find expression and how will the terrible scourge of AIDs affect the sexual element in the way we dress?

Fashion is about Form and Style

Ideas in fashion – as in every area of design – are about the character of physical objects, in this case clothes and accessories. Designers communicate by using aesthetic qualities such as form, colour, texture and pattern. The fundamentals of any design can be analysed under four headings:

Form   This is the shape of a garment, its cut and outline. Because of the way the human eye and brain see the world the silhouette of a person is quickly understood and analysed. Fashion design has always capitalized on this fact, changing people's outline by moving the waistline, emphasizing the bottom, padding up the shoulders and providing exaggerated collars. Or sometimes, as in the tube look of the 1920s, providing a pencil-thin silhouette without bosoms or bottom! In the language of fashion, the form of the garment speaks loudly and makes the major impact which is then enriched and extended by the other elements.

Colour   People feel very strongly about colour. It is an aesthetic quality that can be filled with emotion and symbolic meaning. In fashion, colours change cyclically but there is more to it than that. Within a particular fashion period, the aim may be to get colours to harmonize gently or to clash violently. This use of colour for calmness or energy is closely linked with social change and is a powerful way of communicating ideas. Fashion designers have been among the most sensitive users of colour, exploring new combinations and effects.

Texture and pattern   The feel of cloth, the quality of weave, the printed pattern on fabrics, the character and look of the basic materials – these are the source of endless variation in the design of clothes and accessories. People's appreciation of materials is cyclical, as can be seen in the popularity of vinyl in the sixties and the rediscovery of linen in the eighties. Pattern is full of meaning and it can be used to give a clear and precise message. The notion of the 'pin-stripe suit' has entered the language in powerful contrast to 'blue jeans', spanning the classes by their particular choice of materials. Think, too, of the contrast in meaning between a Laura Ashley skirt, all cottages and roses, and a Mondrian T-shirt, all jazz and modernity. Fashion designers delight in these references and use them deliberately in their work.

Style   By style we mean the effect of the garment as a whole, the way in which the qualities of form, colour, texture and pattern are blended together to produce a particular, unique effect. But style has a further meaning. People are knowledgeable about style. They know, for example, about the Empire line of the 1820s or the bobbed haircut of the 1920s. Locked up inside their heads they have a picture of the Duke of Wellington on his horse with shiny boots, a red jacket and bouncing epaulettes, or they see a cowboy in faded jeans wearing a big sweat-stained black hat. Or again, they see a gangster of the Prohibition era, slouch hat and white spats over highly polished shoes. Designers share this knowledge with their customers and often rediscover or bring back to life aspects of past cycles.

There is a language of style that has been made widely available through education, the media and travel. People living today have access to all the world's cultures, past and present, to an extent that has never existed before. Japanese films have shown us what the *samurai* wore in the fifteenth century and we can see men and women dressed for the desert in Park Lane in London. Today, we can indulge our appreciation of these riches by incorporating them into our own clothes. In one sense, of course, this is sheer fantasy. What we are doing is not very different from what Marie Antoinette did when she dressed up as a shepherdess. But the twentieth century is a century devoted to fantasy as well as to the growth of reason. Our clothes demonstrate this. They are so varied because we live in a period of doubt and questioning. We wonder who we are. We try out different roles and different personalities. Fashion is one of the tools we use in this search. It is the job of fashion designers to deploy the basic elements of form, colour, texture and pattern to create the styles and images that reflect what we feel we want to be.

2 What Do Designers Do?

Although the word 'design' is much used today, its meaning is not always well understood. Design is often seen as something superficial, the icing on the cake, the ingredient added at the last moment to make something sell better or cost more. This is, in fact, the exact opposite of the truth. The work of designers is quite simply to decide how places and products should be. And this means how they should be in *all respects*, not just on the surface.

The Role of Design in Business

In any field, businesses hire designers or have them on their staff to help them make money. Put simplistically, it is the designer's job to imagine future products or services that people will want to buy and so ensure that the business can remain profitable. Designers, like artists, are creative people but their creative skill is geared to an understanding of what the market will demand in the future and how to supply it at a price people will be willing to pay.

There are three main ways in which designers help industry to compete:

1 By conceiving new and better products and services that customers will want to buy.
2 By conceiving new and better places in which to conduct the business. This includes manufacturing facilities as well as places like shops where customers come to buy goods and services.
3 By conceiving new and better communications about and within the business. This will include corporate identity, advertising and every form of graphic design.

The Role of Design in the Fashion Business

Each of the three roles is of vital importance in the fashion industry. It is no use having excellent products if they are badly advertised and marketed. Even the most brilliant advertising will fail, if, when customers come to the company's shops, they are tawdry, inconvenient or out of style. Equally, the best interior design in the world will not be able to sell clothes that people don't like. Each of these aspects of design complements and adds weight to the others.

In the last decade, the concept of design management has emerged to indicate the job of co-ordinating all the design activities of a business so that they create a coherent whole. In any highly competitive field – and fashion is savagely competitive – it is important that the customer can recognize and identify with the distinctive offerings of a particular company. Segmenting the market in this way, by setting out to appeal to the needs and tastes of particular groups of people, is one of the central skills of marketing. Retailer chains like Next and Principles have built success out of meticulous attention to design coherence and identity so that everything – clothes, shop design, window display, advertising, commercials, labelling, house style – is branded as theirs. Franchise companies like Benetton depend even more strongly on house style: it is the key element that binds the individual franchise holders together and gives them a collective identity.

The design of shops and corporate identity for the fashion business is now a big business in its own right. Such work is often commissioned by a fashion company from an independent design consultancy. Firms like Fitch and Co., Michael Peters and Wolff Olins have grown to prominence through their ability to provide the creative flair and management skill needed to carry out wide-ranging design projects, often involving the conversion and development of several hundreds of shops spread over the country. These consultancies employ large numbers of designers but they are generally designers who know about fashion rather than fashion designers. Fitch and Co. employ industrial, interior and graphic designers who, with architects, managers, accountants and quantity surveyors, provide the complete service that the client wants.

In the same way, fashion manufacturers and retailers commission advertising agencies and public relations consultancies to help them market and sell their goods. These companies employ account executives, copy writers, editors, market researchers and market analysts as well as a range of graphic design specialists, photographers and film makers, illustrators and paste-up artists.

Closely connected with the world of advertising, the fashion magazines and fashion coverage on film and television offer a further range of jobs where designers who know about fashion are needed and where experience in fashion design can be put to good use in developing an interesting career.

The Nature of Fashion Design

It is important to be aware of the whole range of design work that is involved in the fashion industry but in this Self-Starter we are mainly concerned with textile, fashion and fashion accessory design. Our focus is on the people who actually conceive and create the products on which the success of the industry ultimately depends. What do they do and how do they do it?

In order to answer this question, it is enlightening and entertaining to step back and put today's highly evolved fashion industry into a brief historical perspective. If we look back 150 years to around 1830 we find that the industry was fragmented into many small businesses and that fashion designers as such did not exist. Even coming up to the beginning of the twentieth century, designers were only just beginning to emerge from the obscurity of being tailors or seamstresses. In his book *Of Human Bondage*, W. Somerset Maugham based one of the characters on Gilbert Clark who began work at Swan and Edgar during the Boer War period. Much later he became a dress designer for Metro-Goldwyn Mayer in the early days of Hollywood. But his beginnings were humble enough:

> After [he] had drawn a successful design for Miss Alice Antonia, the well-known serio-comic, in a show at the Tivoli, the buyer began to treat him a little more deferentially and presently gave him designs to do for two of the country customers. They met with satisfaction. Then he began to speak to his clients of a 'clever young feller, Paris art-student, you know', who worked for him: and soon [Gilbert] ensconced behind a screen, in his shirt-sleeves, was drawing from morning till night. [His] rise from shop-walker to designer had a great effect on the department. He realized that he was an object of envy. But he still received no more than the six shillings a week with which he started.

This is a revealing passage. It demonstrates the cultural domination of Parisian fashion at the turn of the century and it makes clear that clothes for middle-class women were designed as unique one-off garments within the prevailing style. Men's tailors operated in a similar way. In an industry based on handwork and giving highly personal service, designers in the modern sense were simply not required. It needed social, economic and technological change to propel the designer of mass-produced clothes into the centre of the stage.

In contrast to Gilbert, working next door to the showroom and drawing up ideas for immediate translation into garments, the modern designer is part of a huge industry that must begin work two years ahead of the resulting sales. Not only that, but the aim is no longer to produce a single costume for a known customer. What has to be done is to create a design that will catch the imagination and attention of several thousand people.

We tend to think of fashion designers sitting at their drawing boards and having great ideas about a new collection. This idea is wrong in more ways than one. First, because the fashion designer is only one of a number of designers concerned with the development of new styles. The textile designer is equally important and, in fact, begins work many months ahead of the fashion designer. Second, because the shaping of any fashion is done as much by people who know about design as by people who actually wield the pencils and paint-brushes. Colour forecasters, store buyers, textile converters: all these people play a crucial role in the jigsaw of product development in the fashion industry.

Because the industry is so varied in scale and contains so many highly specialist operations, it is hard to generalize about the way it organizes itself. However, it is possible to present a general picture of the stages involved in getting new fashions into the shops. In the example discussed below, we concentrate on mass production because that is the economic heart of the industry today. But it is important to remember that this high street trade is supported by and itself contributes to a diverse and interlocking network of businesses. Manufacturers of accessories, traditional men's tailors, shoe designers, milliners, lingerie designers and manufacturers: all of these and more take inspiration from the general direction of mass fashion and feed back into it their own ideas and approaches.

The Process of Textile and Fashion Design

The fashion jigsaw begins to slot together two years before each new seasonal range of clothing is launched in the high street shops. The appearance of that clothing, including its colour, fabric, shape, style and cut, is the result of a huge collective attempt by almost everyone in the industry to predict, and consequently shape, the future direction of fashion to ensure that their products are the most successful. It is in this crucial area of forecasting what will be in fashion and what will sell that designers have such an important and responsible role to play.

The first major influence on this attempt to predict future fashion trends is an important 'colour meeting' in Paris. Together, leading international yarn dyers, fabric and textile manufacturers, colour consultants, fashion forecasters, fashion and textile designers attempt to decide which colours and textile designs will be in fashion in two years' time. They select up to thirty different colours and divide them into 'trend moods', including a pale mood, neutral mood, dark and bright moods. Depending on the seasons for which the colours are intended, certain colours will predominate: for example, dark reds, greens and burgundies for Autumn; pale pinks, neutrals and browns for Spring. Over the next few months, each manufacturer, colour consultant, fashion forecaster and designer adapts the colour predictions for his or her own end purposes and products.

The fabric and textile manufacturers work with textile technologists and textile designers to produce new yarns and fabrics ready for the European yarn and fabric fairs; the colour consultants and fashion forecasters interpret the new colours in terms of future fashion trends, and pass the ideas on to a wide variety of other textile and clothing manufacturers, retail companies and design studios to develop in their own way; and the fashion designers incorporate the new colours into initial ideas for their own clothing collections, or for those of the manufacturer or company for whom they work. In this way, the latest colour forecasts are soon distributed throughout the fashion network.

The next major influences on the fashion prediction processes are the European yarn and fabric fairs. Here, the fabric and textile manufacturers, textile printers and designers exhibit their latest products, hoping for large orders. The fairs are attended not only by fashion forecasters and designers from clothing manufacturers, retailers and independent 'designer' studios, but also by buyers from major companies and stores. All are anxious to find the latest yarn colours and fabric designs for their new clothing collections now due to be launched in the high street in eighteen months' time. They collect yarn and fabric samples, discuss their initial ideas and requirements with the exhibitors, and return home to begin work on their findings. The 'company' designers and buyers have to present their samples and ideas to their buying, merchandising and quality control teams for approval before initial fabric orders can be placed and work commenced. Independent designers, with only personal taste and style to consider, can place orders immediately and begin work on their new 'designer' collections without the many constraints of 'company' designers. By using smaller – and often more efficient – manufacturers, and a network of skilled freelance sample makers, tailors, jewellers, milliners and shoe makers, designers can produce a new collection of garments and all its accessories in a few months, ready for the international fashion shows. The same process in a large manufacturing or retail company will take the company designer a year to achieve.

The international fashion shows in London, New York, Paris and Milan are the third major influence on the future direction of fashion in the high street shops. These are again attended by fashion forecasters, designers and buyers who are now joined by fashion journalists from leading international fashion magazines and newspapers. Together they scrutinize the 'designer' collections for more new ideas, and frantically monitor everything which might influence future fashion trends. This includes, for example, influential exhibitions, films and theatre, other areas of design, from graphic design to architecture, and general social, economic and cultural trends. After a few weeks of intensive travel and research, the journalists return home to produce articles for their magazines and newspapers, and the forecasters, designers and buyers begin to pull together everything they have seen to create the colours, styles, shapes and cuts of their new clothing ranges, now due to reach the shops in a year's time. They must be absolutely convinced that they are working in the right direction and that they will produce a range of clothing that will sell because now begins the complicated and expensive process of putting the forecasts and ideas into production – of turning them into wearable garments and saleable products. This involves another complex network of people and organizations and, once again, designers have an important and responsible role to play. They must now work with pattern cutters, sample makers, tailors, buyers, merchandisers, quality controllers, textile technologists, marketing executives, public relations experts and sales teams to get the right product in the right place at the right time.

The first stage of the production process involves designers turning their forecasts and findings into initial ideas for garments, including their colours, fabrics, shapes and styles. At the same time they must now constantly bear in mind the commercial requirements of both the company and its customers. If they are designing work clothes or uniforms, their design ideas will be very different from those for evening or formal wear. Designers must also consider whether or not their garments will require special accessories and begin to source (find) the relevant specialist manufacturers and designers. The ideas, in the form of drawings, notes, photographs and yarn and fabric swatches brought back from the fairs, are presented to the buyers who decide which of them are commercially viable. Working closely with textile technologists, the buyers check the quality of the new yarn and fabric swatches, price them, find reliable suppliers and, with a team of merchandisers, order enough fabrics to make up an initial range of sample garments.

Once the designers' ideas are shown to be feasible, it is their job to develop them into detailed working drawings. A skilled pattern cutter and sample maker then turn the drawings into prototype garments so that the designer can see if the ideas work, and adapt them accordingly. The working drawings, fabric samples and prototype garments are then presented to a suitable clothing manufacturer. Guided by the expertise of both the designer and buyer, the manufacturer's production team turns the drawings and prototypes into real sample garments called 'buying samples'. These buying samples must not only meet the approval of the designer and buyer, but also that of textile technologists, quality controllers and merchandisers. This rarely happens first time round. A fabric might not suit a particular style, a garment might not fit properly, a detail might have been missed or a colour might run in the wash! The buying samples are revised and re-made until they meet the requirements of all concerned. At a 'pre-selection meeting', the designer presents all the buying samples to the buyers, quality controllers and merchandisers who together assess their overall sales appeal and predict which of them and how many are most likely to sell and at what price. They select from all the garments a specific range of buying samples and, from their various points of view, suggest how they might be developed and improved.

Guided by these suggestions, the designer, pattern cutters, sample makers, garment technologists and buyers refine and perfect every aspect of the selected garments, including their different sizings, until they look exactly as they will in the high street shops. The final prices are negotiated with the manufacturer and the merchandisers, and the garments are presented at a 'final selection' meeting. At this meeting, the same team, this time including marketing executives, sales staff and public relations people, review and select those garments that will go into full and final production. The merchandisers and quality controllers now take responsibility for the garments' manufacture and distribution to warehouses and shops, freeing the designer to liaise with a third, and final, network of people and organizations. These are the public relations specialists, press officers, fashion journalists, photographers, stylists and illustrators who now publicize and promote the new range of clothing prior to its launch on the market. This is done through special events, such as fashion shows, through fashion magazines, local and national newspapers, radio and television. The designer's moment of truth arrives when, after two years of constant discussion, argument, development work, creative skill, critical judgement, pricing expertise and carefully planned promotion, the clothes finally arrive in the high street shops and the customer does, or does not, buy them! The designer must now liaise with merchandisers, quality controllers and sales staff to monitor sales trends and customer reaction to the new products. This enables repeat orders of successful lines to be made, and decisions taken on those which need to be improved, sold off cheaply or, at worst, withdrawn from sale. Bearing these decisions in mind, the designer can now begin to plan next year's new products, and the whole complex fashion design and production process begins again.

Job Opportunities in the World of Fashion Design

Textile, fashion and accessory design are closely related in the development of a total fashion 'look' but in terms of training, work activities and job opportunities they are each rather different.

Textile Design

Textile manufacturers provide the materials for clothing and furnishing for use in the home and industry. These are utilitarian and decorative. Textile design falls into two divisions:

1 *Printed textiles and surface pattern*   The pattern is put on to the surface of the material, for example by printing or embroidery.

2 *Woven and knitted textiles*   Here the design is a part of the construction of the material, for example by the interweaving of fibres of different colours and textures.

In textile design, the ability to draw and to use colour and texture is most important. It is also necessary to have a good knowledge of the machinery and techniques used in the industry, where computer-aided design and manufacture are now becoming commonplace. A good business sense and awareness of how textiles meet commercial needs is also required.

Textiles provide the opportunity to work in a variety of ways. Designers may be freelance serving mass production, work in a company or as designer-makers producing small quantities of textiles in their own right.

Possible job titles related to textile design

> Textile designer (print, stitch or weave)
> Knitwear designer
> Fashion forecaster
> Colour consultant
> Design co-ordinator
> Studio designer
> Studio manager
> Textile technician
> Design manager
> Textile buyer
> Quality controller
> Textile researcher
> Textile librarian
> Textile conservation

Fashion Design

Fashion designers must not only be imaginative and produce new ideas, they must also understand the craftsmanship and technology involved in making clothes. They need to understand the potential and limitations of textiles, how patterns are graded and cut and the methods used in constructing and making garments. They must be aware of the interaction between markets, prices, costs and technology.

Fashion design falls into three divisions:

1 *High fashion, couture houses* Here exclusive clothes are designed and made and marketed directly under the direction of the designer or design house.

2 *Mass production* Clothes are designed for the high street shops. The designers involved may be freelance, employed by the manufacturer or part of a large retailer's design team.

3 *Designer-maker* Clothes are designed and made sometimes for direct sale in small quantities, sometimes for individuals and sometimes as prototypes for quantity production.

Possible job titles related to fashion design

Fashion designer (menswear, womenswear, childrenswear)

Fashion forecaster

Fashion design consultant

Colour consultant

Design co-ordinator

Quality controller

Design manager

Retail shop manager

Fashion buyer

Fashion journalist

Fashion illustrator

Theatre, film or TV costume design

Pattern cutter/grader

Fashion merchandiser

Fashion press officer

Fashion photographer

Display designer

Accessory Design

The fashion accessory industry is extremely diverse. It frequently uses traditional means of production that have to be well understood by the designer. Shoes, for example, are complex three-dimensional forms and the 'know-how' about their construction is very specialized. Designers therefore tend to specialize in a particular area or aspect. The following can be included in the accessory industry:

Shoes

Hosiery

Millinery

Lingerie

Bags and belts

Gloves

Jewellery

In each of these fields there exists a wide range of prices, quantities and markets. Designers may work for a large manufacturing company, be part of a design/production team, or operate on a freelance basis. Accessories offer particularly good opportunities for designer-makers because there is a good demand for exclusive pieces to add individuality and style.

Part 2　　The Industry in Action

Three Case Studies

How does the fashion industry actually operate? The best way to understand this is by looking in more detail at the day-to-day work of specific organizations and their staff. In this part of the book we take three well-known companies, very varied in scale, product and target markets. We describe their approach to the business of design and then we talk to key members of staff to find out what they do.

3 Next Ltd

Next has been acclaimed as 'the retail phenomenon of the 1980s'. Considering such acclaim, Next could be seen as having surprising origins. Its parent company, J. Hepworth & Sons, Gentleman's Outfitters, was a well-established and respected, but slightly old-fashioned retail company with a reputation for producing good quality menswear and tailoring. In 1981, a new and dynamic management team identified a gap in the retail market for good quality, stylish womenswear at competitive prices. An existing chain of high street stores was purchased and George Davis was appointed as merchandise director. His role was to launch the concept and develop the range of womenswear. Almost overnight, seventy new womenswear shops appeared in major British high streets under the memorable and adaptable trade name 'Next'. The shops, with their distinctive house style, inviting window displays and imaginatively designed interiors caused quite a stir among competitors and customers alike, as did their colour co-ordinated and high quality merchandise. The shops were an immediate and overwhelming success. In only four years, George Davis was promoted to chief executive and won the 1985 *Guardian* Young Businessman of the Year Award.

Under George Davis's inspired and, at times, daring guidance, the concept of Next took off. Its product range increased to include menswear, childrenswear, shoes, accessories, jewellery, lingerie and homeware. Its retail outlets and marketing activities expanded to include individual shops, each with a distinctive but related house style and specializing in one product range; mini-department stores comprising different product departments, cafés and florists; Department X, large and ultra modern outlets stocking Next's complete range of merchandise; and a 'home-shopping' mail-order service covering clothing, accessories and homeware.

Above all, Next's range of customers increased, from the twenty-five- to forty-year-old women at whom the original womenswear range was aimed, to women, men and children of all shapes, sizes, lifestyles and incomes. The whole 'Next phenomenon' soon caused nervous competitors to re-examine their products and change their ways. So what and who has created the 'Next phenomenon'? As suggested earlier, two ingredients make or break a company, especially in the fashion industry – its products and the people who create and market those products.

In the case of Next, two main elements contribute to the success of its products. The first is the management team's ability, under the initial guidance of George Davis, constantly to increase and improve the product range and, in so doing, reach a much wider range of customers than many other similar organizations:

> Our key aim has been to develop a wide portfolio of products with a high level of recognition and acceptability by the consumer.

This ability is most clearly shown in the development of Next's first womenswear range. This was initially aimed at a cross-section of twenty-five- to forty-year-old women who were thought to require good quality, classic and comfortable clothing suitable for wearing at work, at home with a family, or on social occasions. However, it was soon apparent that the range was purchased by a much wider variety of customers, including teenage girls wanting high fashion garments, young women wanting 'designer looks' and older women wanting smart, co-ordinated garments. For this reason, and to increase its marketing opportunities and prevent every Next customer from looking the same, the womenswear range was expanded and diversified into three ranges: 'Next Collection' for the classic, stylish look; 'Next Too' for the more casual look and 'Next Originals' for a high fashion look:

> The development of a broad product range has necessarily been viewed in conjunction with the vital need to preserve exclusivity. Emphasis on exclusivity has led to the creation of separate and distinctive ladieswear ranges.

The new ranges were marketed either in existing mini-department stores or in their own distinctive shops which soon attracted their own clientele and, as a result, did not affect the sales of the others. This successful marketing strategy was soon applied to other Next product ranges, including menswear and childrenswear.

The second element which contributes towards the success of Next's products is the total commitment throughout the whole company, from shop-floor staff to senior executives, to the design and manufacture of good quality products. This also highlights the remaining key to a company's success – the nature and quality of its people:

> Next believes in people. Its belief expresses itself in two particular ways. Firstly a working environment is created free from 'red tape' which enables talented people to express themselves. This is particularly vital in a company whose success is based on managing innovation. Creative people need the scope to be able to express themselves . . . People are the cornerstone of our business and our belief in them, both individually and collectively, is fundamental to our future growth.

The core of Next's own in-house product design and development team consists of several groups of skilled and talented designers, buyers, merchandisers and quality assurers, the heads of which are part of the company's senior management team. Together, they create, design and oversee manufacture and quality, and distribute the company's products. This gives the team, especially the buyers and merchandisers, a much more creative, innovative and influential role than in many other companies who, rather than create their own products, rely on outside designers and manufacturers to do it for them, or select their products from existing ones. Although this gives the Next team the exciting opportunity to produce exactly what the company and its customers require, such an approach demands complete co-operation throughout the design and development teams, and an excellent working relationship with manufacturers and suppliers:

> As a retail group we have always had a strong belief in the special partnership that exists between manufacturing and ourselves.

So strong is this belief, that Next now owns several of its major manufacturers, investing both money and expertise in factories in Britain, the Far East and Mauritius.

Each group within Next's in-house design and development team has its own distinct responsibilities but, as suggested earlier, they work as part of an integrated and co-operative team. The buyers and designers are responsible for the creation and design of the company's products, and for ensuring that the manufacturer produces exactly what is required at the right quality and price. The merchandisers are responsible for ensuring that the right quantities of products are produced at the right price, and that they always reach their destination, whether factory, warehouse or shop, on time. The quality assurers are responsible for ensuring that the quality of the products is constantly maintained or improved.

The commitment to design and quality at Next does not end with the design and development team at the company's head office. It continues into the most crucial of places, the shops themselves. Here, the shop managers take great care to display the new products to their best advantage, and to monitor customer reaction to them. No matter how talented or skilled the team who have created the products, the moment of truth only arrives when the customer does or does not buy them, and an untidy display or badly lit shop could prevent them from doing so.

Next People and their Jobs

Director Designate of Buying

Alison is the product director of ladieswear at Next's head office.

Alison always wanted to be a fashion designer, but received little guidance at school. On leaving, she did a two-year foundation course in art and design, followed by a degree course in fashion and textile design at Nottingham Polytechnic. The degree course helped Alison to develop her ideas and introduced her to almost every area of fashion design, including ladies-, mens- and childrenswear, knitwear, printed and woven textiles, although she chose to specialize in menswear. Looking back Alison feels that the course did not have enough industrial and commercial content. Though her ideas were often exciting, they were not always commercially viable.

On graduating, Alison was determined to gain more industrial experience, and immediately joined Courtaulds as a ladies' jersey-wear designer. She worked directly with experienced designers, pattern cutters, machinists and production teams, and liaised with large commercial companies, including Marks and Spencer. This introduced Alison to the more commercial side of the fashion industry and she soon learnt how to turn her ideas into viable products required by both the company and its clients.

With such invaluable experience, Alison moved on to set up a new design studio for a sportswear manufacturer. Her role was to appoint a small team of designers, pattern cutters, sample machinists and production staff, and supervise every stage of manufacture, from initial drawings and costings to cloth sourcing and production schedules. Under Alison's guidance, the new team produced practical but stylish ranges of sportswear for leading companies. From sportswear, Alison turned to designing 'high fashion' shirts for a small family firm which supplied high street chain stores. As most of the firm's manufacturers were based overseas, Alison often had to liaise with them at a distance. Her working drawings, used by the manufacturers to produce the finished shirts, had to be detailed and accurate because she was not cutting the patterns herself and other people would have to interpret her work. A linguistic misunderstanding or a missed detail on the drawing could result in mistakes on the final garments and financial losses for both manufacturers and shirt company.

Unexpectedly, Alison was invited to become an assistant buyer for menswear at Next's new head office. At this stage, the company had no in-house design team and was recruiting candidates with a strong design background and varied industrial experience. Alison joined, finding her knowledge of both design and manufacturing invaluable. Gradually, she progressed to her present role of product director for Next's ladieswear.

Alison is responsible for the success or failure of all Next's ladieswear products, including Next Collection, Next Originals, cosmetics and lingerie. She heads a large team of over sixty buyers and designers who work very closely with the merchandisers, quality assurers and sales teams. Together they create and develop high quality and stylish merchandise at competitive prices.

Alison's main role begins each season when her team of buyers and designers sit down with the merchandisers to plan what kind of merchandise will be sold in Next's shops and Next Directory mail-order catalogue in a year's time. The members of each group outline their ideas and suggestions based on their particular area of expertise. The buyers outline what kind of merchandise they want to develop for their new product ranges. The designers present their initial design proposals, inspired by a variety of sources including a review of last season's major fashion influences, current fashion magazines, films, exhibitions, and visits abroad to leading fashion stores and fashion shows. Based on a careful analysis of the previous year's sales figures, the merchandisers predict what kind of merchandise is most likely to sell, and at what price. It is Alison's task as product director to assess all these ideas and suggestions and, from them, develop a 'range control plan'. This details exactly what kind of merchandise, and at what selling price, Alison wants to include in the new range of Next ladieswear and lingerie. The range might include, for example, three distinct fashion 'looks', each with several different styles of skirts, trousers and jackets in various fabrics and colourways; a range of co-ordinating knitwear and blouses, and a complementary selection of shoes and accessories. The 'range control plan' is crucial. It forms the basis of all Alison and her team's product design and development work over the next few months and, consequently, determines what kind of merchandise eventually reaches Next's shops and its customers.

Once the 'range control plan' is finalized, Alison and her team of buyers and designers attend yarn, fabric and fashion shows throughout the world. There they observe future fashion trends, check that their own 'range control plan' is in line with current ideas, collect suitable yarn and fabric samples and make contact with relevant manufacturers and suppliers. On their return, the design manager and her design team, now confident that their ideas are following the latest fashion trends, formulate in detail proposals for the new range's main 'looks', including their colours, fabrics, shapes and styles. These are then presented to Alison and her buyers who decide which of the design team's proposals fit in best with the 'range control plan' and can therefore be developed into the kinds of merchandise they, and Next's customers, require.

Working closely with the quality assurers and laboratory technicians, Alison and her buyers check the quality of all the new yarn and fabric samples brought back from the fairs. Only if the samples pass Next's own stringent testing standards will Alison buy the yarns or fabrics. Once the design team's proposals are shown to be feasible, they develop them into detailed working drawings. These, together with accurate specifications, fabric samples and prototype garments made up in Next's own sample room, are presented to the manufacturer. Guided by the buyers and designers, the manufacturer's development team turns the drawings and specifications into sample garments called buying samples which, along with detailed costings, are then submitted for selection.

At a 'pre-selection meeting', the buyers and designers present all the buying samples for a management review by Alison, her fellow directors, including the design director and the technical services director, and the merchandisers who, as a team, assess the samples' commercial potential. Everything about the samples is discussed, including their cost, the availability of their fabrics, minimum quantities, production lead times, and so on. Eventually a specific range of garments is selected for further development: the range not only meets everyone's criteria, but also fits into the previously arranged 'range control plan'.

Guided by the discussions at the 'pre-selection meeting', the buyers and designers now set to work refining and perfecting every aspect of the garments until they look exactly as they will in Next's shops or in the Next Directory mail-order catalogue. The final prices are negotiated with the manufacturers, and the range is ready to be presented at the 'final selection' meeting. At this meeting, the same team review the perfected garments and make a final selection of those that will go into production. The merchandisers and quality assurers now take the main responsibility for the garments' manufacture and distribution, freeing Alison to plan next year's range and fulfil her many other duties. These include liaison with the publicity department to promote new ranges in the press and on television, visits to Next stores to assess the overall visual impact of a new range, and customer reaction to it; visits to overseas suppliers; the monitoring of sales trends throughout the season; interviewing and training new staff, and so on!

Alison's job is highly responsible. If, through inefficient management or poor motivation, Alison's buying team make a wrong decision, it can have serious commercial implications for the whole company. Alison must ensure that this does not happen. The job is also demanding, requiring energy and total commitment to the company. Long hours and frequent working weekends leave little time for home and social life. But Alison loves her job, finding it varied and challenging. She is well paid and works with friendly and enthusiastic staff.

When recruiting trainee buyers, Alison looks for candidates with a strong personal style, a genuine interest in fashion and design and an ability to work in and share responsibility within a team. Her current buying team have come from a variety of backgrounds. Some have degrees in fashion design, marketing or business studies. Others have worked their way up through the company, perhaps by starting out on the shop floor, or by moving across from another department. Whatever their backgrounds, all Alison's buyers underwent Next's own training course.

Design Manager

Ann-Marie is a design manager in charge of a small team of fashion designers at Next's head office.

Ann-Marie always wanted to be a fashion designer. She trained at Middlesex Polytechnic and the Royal College of Art in London where, in her final year, she specialized in knitwear design. On leaving college, she went to work as a knitwear designer for a Paris company. The job was not to her liking and she soon returned to Britain, very disillusioned.

Jobs were few at this time, so Ann-Marie set up as a freelance knitwear designer and maker. She sold her first collection to a fashionable London shop which gave her so many orders that she could not keep up. Despite the success of the collection, a year of overwork, long hours and poor business knowledge led her to look for a 'proper job'. She joined a company which designed and produced knitwear for several high street shops. A year later she had another attempt at freelancing, designing and knitting exclusive collections for individual and highly fashionable London shops. The same problems arose and she went to work for a designer she greatly admired – Sally Tuffin of Foale and Tuffin. There, Ann-Marie learnt many of the technical and commercial aspects of the fashion business including fabric sourcing and buying, pattern cutting, dealing with buyers and suppliers, and so on. After two years, Ann-Marie joined a fashion consultancy where she managed the fashion design department and handled huge overseas contracts. Five years later, she was invited to join another consultancy to set up and develop a new womenswear department. She remained there for a further five years. Although these jobs were creative and rewarding, she still wanted to increase her commercial experience.

On seeing an advertisement for posts with Next, she joined the company as a buyer/designer. At this stage, there was no formal design team and Ann-Marie worked solely as a buyer. Frustrated by long hours and lack of design input, she returned to freelance designing, eventually working full time for one of her clients. Meanwhile, Next had developed its own design team and invited her to return as a design manager, her present role.

The design manager's main role starts at the beginning of each fashion season when, together with her co-design manager and design director, she decides what will be in fashion in a year's time. The three review last season's best-selling garments and decide which of them should be modified to continue into the following year, study the latest fashion magazines, travel abroad to research new looks in leading fashion stores and, where possible, accompany the buying team to fabric and yarn fairs throughout the world. The design team then develop their ideas on colour, shape, style and fabric into proposals for several different fashion looks. They constantly bear in mind the requirements of Next's customers and the company's distinctive style.

The proposals for the new looks are then presented to the buying team. They decide which of the design proposals fit best into their pre-arranged 'range control plan', and select those which can be developed into the types of garments they and Next's customers require. It is now the buying team's main responsibility to turn the chosen design proposals into such garments. They find relevant yarn and fabric suppliers and discuss how to develop the garments with the design team who now produce detailed working drawings and specifications. These, together with fabric samples and, in many cases, a made-up prototype garment produced by the pattern cutters and machinists in the sample room, show exactly what each garment will look like. The buyers then take these to the manufacturer who, under their guidance, produces an initial range of sample garments known as 'buying samples'. These samples must not only meet with the approval of the design team, but also with that of the buying team. This rarely happens first time round. For example, a fabric might not suit a particular style or may not pass the quality assurers' rigorous laboratory tests. The samples are revised and remade until they fulfil the requirements of all concerned. At a 'pre-selection meeting' the design and buying teams present all the buying samples for a management review by the directors and merchandisers. Together, they select specific ranges of garments to go into production. These meetings take place twice – once for Next's retail range and once for the Next Directory range.

The buyers and design team then work closely with the manufacturers to modify and perfect the selected garments for a 'final selection meeting' . After detailed discussions, the directors, designers, buyers and merchandisers select the final range of garments that will be manufactured and distributed to Next's stores or mail-order Directory. Ann-Marie's role as design manager has come full circle. She must now begin to think about next year's looks.

Ann-Marie's job is highly responsible. Working to constant deadlines, she often has to make important decisions under great pressure. A misguided prediction about next season's 'looks' or a badly briefed design team could lead to serious financial losses. She sees such responsibility as a challenge. She enjoys working with a team of enthusiastic young designers and finds it rewarding to see their designs in the high street. When recruiting a new designer, she looks for someone with individuality, a sound design training and commercial knowledge, a willingness to adapt and an ability to work in a team. With such qualities, a young designer at Next may well see his or her designs worn on the high street within a year of joining the company.

Merchandise Manager

Alan is the merchandise manager for menswear at Next's head office.

Alan has worked in the fashion and textiles industry ever since leaving school. His first job was in the fabric export department at Tootals. While there, Alan heard that J. Hepworth & Sons, the men's outfitters, offered a training scheme for trainee buyers, one of the few companies to do so. He joined it, but discovered that no such formal scheme existed. Alan was placed with a senior buyer for a season and expected to learn everything as he went along. This required initiative and motivation.

At this stage, Hepworth's buying team did everything now done by merchandisers. They set budgets, placed contracts and orders with suppliers, distributed goods to the shops and so on. This was not the most efficient use of their time so the new role of merchandiser was created, and Alan became one.

In 1983, George Davis integrated Hepworth's with Next, ready for the launch of Next for Men. Alan joined a new team of buyers and merchandisers and moved to Next's head office. He soon progressed to a senior merchandiser and, most recently, merchandise manager for menswear.

The main role of Alan's merchandise department is to ensure that the correct quantities of stock are ordered and distributed to arrive in the right place at the right time. At the beginning of each season, Alan calculates the menswear budgets for the following season. He does this by analysing the previous sales figures and forecasting future sales. Once the budgets have been agreed with the finance department, Alan's merchandisers work closely with the menswear buyers and designers.

At a 'pre-selection meeting', the buyers and designers present all their sample garments (buying samples) to the merchandisers. By interpreting last season's sales figures, the merchandisers assess the overall sales appeal of the garments and predict which specific ranges are most likely to sell, and at what price. Guided by this information, the buyers and designers develop and improve these ranges for a 'final selection meeting'. At this stage, the buyers, designers, merchandisers and quality assurers make a final selection of the range of garments that will go into production.

Alan's next task is to divide his budget across the final range of garments, allocating a certain percentage to each style. This results in a 'range plan' which helps Alan to calculate the initial quantities of each style to be produced.

By now, the buyers have negotiated the style and price of each garment with the manufacturer. It is the merchandise department's responsibility to buy fabrics, ensure they reach the manufacturers on time, and discuss quantities and delivery dates. From then on, the department's main task is 'progress chasing'. They must monitor the progress of the garments being manufactured, ensure that deadlines are met and that stock arrives in the warehouse on time, ready to be distributed to the shops. Computerized information about each shop enables Alan to construct a plan showing the exact range and quantity of styles that each shop will receive.

Throughout the season, Alan's merchandise department monitors and analyses sales and customer reaction to the range. This enables repeat orders to be made where necessary and, after discussion with the buyers, decisions to be taken on styles to be withdrawn from the range. At the end of each season, the merchandisers and buyers agree which styles will continue into next season, and which will be sold off in end-of-season sales, and the whole cycle begins again!

Alan's job is not merely one of 'number-crunching' and stock control. At Next, it is creative, demanding and varied. One minute he could be discussing the style of a garment with the design team, and the next flying abroad to meet a manufacturer. Alan enjoys working closely with many different and enthusiastic people throughout the company, from the financial directors to the buyers and quality controllers. He finds it exciting constantly to be planning ahead and making influential decisions. But such a job requires motivation and complete commitment to the company and its products. Hours are long, leaving little time or energy for life beyond work.

Next provides a good training scheme and excellent career opportunities for trainee merchandisers. When appointing new recruits, Alan looks for initiative, ambition, numeracy, an ability to take decisions and work in a team, and a genuine interest in the fashion industry.

Technical Services Director

Cedric is the technical services director for Next. He did an economics degree with a textiles option at Leeds University. During the course, he became far more interested in textiles than economics and stayed on to do a masters degree. He researched into various technical aspects of textile design and production, including the effect of changing climates on garments for the International Wool Secretariat.

On leaving Leeds University, Cedric joined Daks Simpson as a menswear manufacturer. He worked on the factory floor as a general manager, and supervised the production of men's jackets from start to finish. Such direct industrial experience proved invaluable after a research-based background. In return, Cedric introduced several new production techniques to the company.

From Daks Simpson, Cedric moved on to J. Hepworth & Sons, an established men's outfitters and Next's parent company. At this stage, George Davis was appointed as merchandise director to develop and launch the Next concept. He did this so successfully that, from being a small part of Hepworth's, Next eventually took over. Cedric was retained for his technical expertise and appointed technical services director for all Next's products.

The technical services director must ensure that the high quality of Next's products, the basis of their success, is always maintained or improved. He heads a team of quality assurers and technicians. Together, the team oversee the production of all Next's products. They check them at every stage of manufacture and solve any technical or quality-control problem that may arise. This includes carrying out initial laboratory tests on fabrics and yarns, helping the design and buying teams to solve problems of garment construction, advising manufacturers on how to improve their production quality, and so on.

The technical services director's role begins when the buyers and design managers return from the yarn and fabric fairs with their samples. His technical team assess the quality of the samples by subjecting them to rigorous testing procedures. They then advise the buyers and designers on which of the yarns and fabrics to use in the development of their new garment ranges. If the samples are from an unfamiliar supplier, the technical services director will visit their factory to assess their production quality. Once satisfied, the relevant yarns are ordered and sent for dyeing and fabrics are booked, ready to make up an initial range of sample garments in one size. To this end, the buyers and designers develop their ideas into detailed working drawings to show exactly what each finished garment will look like. The manufacturer then uses these to produce the sample garments, known as 'buying samples'. These are seldom correct first time. The technical services director and his team must check the size, fit, style and construction of each and discuss with the buyer and manufacturer any changes that are required. The buying samples are then re-made until they are perfect, and used by the manufacturer to draw up a provisional size chart.

In addition to size, fit, style and construction, the colour of each buying sample must be laboratory tested for colour-fastness and colour continuity. Once the colour meets the approval of both the technical services director and the buyer, 'bulk dyeing' of the fabrics and yarns for the final production run can begin. As a precaution, the first 'lot' of dyed fabric or yarn is sent to the laboratory to ensure that it matches the buying sample. If it does, the 'dye lot' will become standard and all subsequent dye lots will need to match it to be accepted. This guarantees colour continuity throughout all subsequent production runs. These laboratory tests also enable the technical services director and his team to devise washing or care instructions to go on the label of every garment. Once the buying samples meet all the technical requirements the manufacturer makes one garment of each size that is to be produced. The technical services director then tries each size garment on a range of same sized but differently shaped people – a small size twelve, a tall size twelve, a broad-shouldered size twelve, and so on. If the garment fits all these people it is approved and a complete 'size set chart' drawn up ready for the pilot production run. This enables the technical services director and his team to solve any quality control or technical problems before the final production run begins.

Throughout the final production run, the technical services director and his team of quality assurers visit the manufacturers to check the quality of the garments at every stage. All completed and boxed stock is given a further 'pre-delivery' check before it is dispatched to a Next warehouse and then on to the stores.

But the technical services director's role does not end once the finished stock reaches the shops. He must now liaise with the merchandising and customer services departments to analyse why customers return garments or complain about them. If the problem is one of quality – a broken zip or crooked hem – he must work with his technicians, the designer, the buyer, the supplier and the manufacturer to put it right and ensure that the same problem does not happen again.

Cedric's role as a technical services director is highly responsible. The quality of all Next's products depends on his technical, commercial and managerial expertise. This includes his ability to select, train and supervise a skilled team of quality assurers; his ability to liaise with designers, buyers, suppliers, manufacturers and customers; and above all, his ability constantly to analyse and solve problems under great pressure. When appointing new trainee technicians and quality assurers, Cedric and his team look for candidates with a sound training in textile technology and a strong interest in fashion design; some managerial and industrial experience on which Next's own training scheme can build; an ability to work under pressure and an attitude compatible to that of the whole company.

Sample Maker

Pauline works as a sample machinist in the sample studio at Next's head office.

Pauline received no formal training but since leaving school has worked as a machinist in many areas of the fashion industry, including children's tailored clothing, knitwear and lingerie. Such mixed experience not only taught Pauline how to construct all kinds of garments, but also the ways in which different fabrics behave when turned into garments. For example, making up a child's tailored tweed coat demands a very different approach from that required for making up a loose-fitting silk dressing gown.

Pauline's varied industrial background made her an ideal candidate to join Next's sample studio. Pauline works in a small team of highly skilled pattern cutters and graders, cloth cutters and machinists. The pattern cutters each received a formal technical training at college while the machinists, like Pauline, came from industry. In addition, there are always several trainees in the studio to ensure that young, skilled technicians are available should someone move on.

The sample studio team work closely with the designers and buyers, providing them with a vital technical back-up service.

Working from the designer's drawings and specifications, Pauline and her colleagues turn them into garments. They produce a paper pattern in sample size twelve, cut the sample cloth sourced by the buyers at the fabric fairs and make up an initial prototype garment. This enables the designer and buyer to see if their ideas really work. Pauline can advise the designer on any technical problems she may have encountered while making the garment. In conjunction with the technical services department and the quality assurance team, Pauline can then suggest ways in which the problems might be solved. Such problems could include, for example, a cloth which does not hang well in a certain style; a cloth which is difficult to handle; a style which is too complicated to produce or which will not work in larger or smaller sizes, and so on. This advice is invaluable. It enables the designer and buyer to modify and correct their drawings, and Pauline to make up the revised garment before involving the actual manufacturer. Once all the problems are resolved, the sample garment and drawings are given to the manufacturer's production team who use them to produce their own sample garment, known as a 'buying sample'. This helps the designers, buyers and quality assurers at Next to ensure that the manufacturer is capable of producing exactly what they require. Later in the production process, Pauline and her colleagues help the designers and buyers to refine and perfect the 'buying samples' ready to be presented at the 'final selection meeting'. This is the last opportunity for everyone involved to review the garments before they go into final production.

In addition, Pauline and her team make up sample garments for several other important purposes. These include 'press samples' borrowed by fashion editors to photograph and feature in their magazines and newspapers; fashion show samples to promote a new range; and catalogue samples, most of the garments depicted in the Next Directory. In each case, the promotion and publicity of a new range of garments and the preparation of the Directory take place so far in advance that the final manufactured garments do not exist and accurate samples are used instead. This can sometimes lead to problems if, for example, a sample is shown in a fabric or colourway that is changed in the final range.

Pauline enjoys being part of a skilled team which provides such an important back-up service to the designers and buyers. She finds it challenging to put their ideas into practice, especially if the designer requires something that, from experience, Pauline knows will not work; and constantly exciting to discover what will be in fashion in a year's time. When taking on trainees, Pauline and her colleagues look for co-operative and adaptable candidates with either a sound technical training in garment construction, or wide industrial experience.

Shop Manageress

Julie manages a large Next store in a busy Nottingham shopping centre. The store sells the complete range of Next's products and also has a bustling café. Julie and her management team have to ensure that every aspect of the store runs smoothly, that the sales staff are friendly and efficient and that, above all, the customers are satisfied.

On leaving school, Julie began her career as a sales assistant in the rainwear department of a Kendall's store. She had no formal training but learnt the basics of selling as she went along. In 1982, Julie joined Next as a sales consultant, shortly after the company's launch. A twelve-week induction course introduced Julie to every aspect of her new job. This included sales skills – how to present yourself, sell your company's products and deal with the customers; and shop-floor skills – how to use a cash-till, look after stock, do stock control, supervise fitting rooms and so on. Taking advantage of Next's own management training schemes, available to all ambitious shop-floor staff, Julie soon progressed from sales consultant up to store manageress, her present role.

Julie's working day begins when she and her staff take delivery of new stock and check it in against their stock-control sheets. They also calculate the previous day's sales figures and the weekly takings to date. There is then a daily meeting before the store opens to the public. Julie's staff are given all the information they will need for the day or week ahead. This might include details of special sales promotions, departmental sales targets, and a chance to discuss any problems. This meeting also helps the staff to feel that they are an important and valued part of the whole company. Once the store has opened, Julie does a detailed 'floorwalk' in the store and café, and behind the scenes in areas of the store which the public do not see. She ensures that the shop staff and everything in the shop looks well presented, and that such things as fire exits and security alarm systems are in good working order. She then goes to her office to oversee a wide variety of administrative and managerial matters. These might include dealing with customer queries and job applications, answering letters, double-checking stock-control details, organizing stock deliveries, interviewing new staff, solving day-to-day problems, attending meetings, entertaining visiting personnel from head office, and so on. After a short lunch break, usually spent with her colleagues in the office, Julie returns to the shop floor to serve customers and assist sales staff. After the store has closed, Julie and her staff shut down the cash-tills and prepare the day's takings so that they can immediately be delivered to the bank. She then does a second 'floorwalk' to ensure that everything is ready for the next day. Finally she returns to her office and helps her staff to feed the day's sales figures into a centralized computer.

Julie's job is well paid and rewarding. It is also very demanding, requiring commitment, stamina and an ability to work with people and cope with constant problems. When appointing new sales consultants, Julie looks for lively and presentable people with ambition and a genuine interest in Next, its customers and its products. The company's comprehensive training schemes and career structure mean that, like Julie, a junior sales consultant can become a top manager, provided he or she has personality and motivation.

4 Marks and Spencer PLC

Like Next, the Marks and Spencer store with its distinctive green and gold house style is a familiar and welcoming sight in almost every British high street or shopping centre. Unlike Next, Marks and Spencer PLC is a long-established company whose reputation for quality, value and reliability, built up over more than a hundred years, has made it into something of a great British institution. The phrases 'M & S' or 'Marks and Sparks' are part of everyday vocabulary, and practically everyone, from politicians to pensioners, has shopped there at some time, whether it be exclusively for socks, or for the weekly groceries.

For such a well-known, popular and successful institution, Marks and Spencer PLC, like Next, has surprising origins. In 1882 Michael Marks, a young Russian refugee, arrived in the north-east of England and began to sell habadashery to local villagers from a tray carried around his neck. In 1884, Marks borrowed five pounds from Isaac Dewhirst, a local wholesaler whose family firm still supplies the company, to set up a stall on Leeds market. Marks's wares cost no more than a penny and his slogan became, 'Don't ask the price, it's a penny,' thus establishing the idea of a fixed 'price point'. By 1894, Marks had eight stalls in the north of England and, needing money for expansion, formed a partnership with Tom Spencer, a cashier from Isaac Dewhirst's. Marks and Spencer was born.

By 1901, the partners had twenty-four stalls in various covered markets and twelve shops in major cities, including Leeds, Cardiff, Manchester, Bath and London. In 1903, the partnership was made into a limited company and, in 1911, Marks's eldest son, Simon Marks, was appointed a director. Together with his brother-in-law, Israel Sieff, Simon Marks set about shaping the future destiny of Marks and Spencer and introduced several long-term company policies which are still in operation today. In 1924, the company adopted the important policy of whenever possible buying direct from British manufacturers, many of whom continue to supply it. This not only enabled the company to monitor closely the quality of its products, but also to establish excellent and close working relationships with leading manufacturers – something of which the company is still extremely proud. In 1926, Marks and Spencer became a public company with 125 stores selling clothes, food and homeware which cost no more than five shillings. In 1928, the now familiar 'St Michael' trademark, representing quality and value, was introduced on products manufactured to the company's own strict specifications and standards. In only four years, all Marks and Spencer's major company policies had been put into operation.

The 1930s saw a period of continued expansion and an emphasis on improving the quality of both the company's products and the working conditions and, consequently, morale and loyalty, of its staff – the two ingredients vital to the success of every retail company. To this end, Marks and Spencer set up its own quality control laboratories to test its products and a welfare department to provide a wide range of services for its staff, many of which laid the foundations for those still provided today. These include above-average salaries; discounts on company merchandise; pension, savings and profit-sharing schemes; a medical, dental and hairdressing service; subsidized meals and good holiday leave.

By the 1950s Marks and Spencer had become a leader in the field of food hygiene and, as wartime restrictions were lifted, set about improving its existing stores and building new ones. During the 1970s, the company began trading in Canada, France and Belgium, and the Republic of Ireland, winning the Queen's Award for Export Achievement. By the mid-1980s it had set up the first 'edge-of-town' superstores, 'satellite' stores specializing in one area of merchandise – for example, childrenswear; its own credit card scheme and computerized distribution network; and, most recently, stores in America and Hong Kong. Not surprisingly, Marks and Spencer PLC is now Britain's leading high street retailer and one of its top ten companies with an annual multi-million pound turnover. It has over 500 stores worldwide, each of which stocks a wide range of mass-produced but high quality and competitively priced merchandise. This appeals to a huge variety and number of customers, and includes womenswear, menswear, childrenswear and leisurewear; lingerie and underwear; cosmetics and toiletries; shoes and accessories; books; stationery; homeware and furniture; food and drink.

So what has made Marks and Spencer such a long-lasting, popular and successful retail company? There are several important factors. The first is the company's understanding of and reaction to major changes in retailing which have taken place throughout its history and, in particular, over the last few years. The company has realized that competitors of all kinds and operating on every scale have changed their approach towards their customers and their products. Gone are the days of old-fashioned stores in which shopping was a chore. Stores of every kind, from Next to Top Shop, have become more exciting, enticing and pleasing places in which to spend time and, to the retailers' delight, money. With increased competition from each other and from abroad, their products are better designed, more varied and influenced to a much greater degree by style and fashion than ever before. Marks and Spencer has realized that to remain a market leader it must keep up with, if not ahead of, such changes. This is illustrated in recent upmarket publicity and promotion campaigns in which the company's latest womenswear ranges have been photographed by top fashion photographers and featured in leading magazines including *Vogue* and *The Clothes Show*. Like the old-fashioned stores, gone are the days of 'Good old M & S' when their clothing always represented quality and value but frequently lacked style. The company must continue to know its products, their place in the rapidly changing retail market and its customers inside out.

The second reason for the company's long-standing success is its commitment, like Next, to the people who design, select, manufacture and market its products, and to the people who buy and use these products. Over the years, the company has established a large and complex team of skilled people, including designers, pattern makers, textile technologists, buyers, merchandisers, manufacturers and marketing experts to develop a range of products that they know, from careful research and commercial experience, their customers really want:

> It is people: public tastes and public requirements on the one hand and the skills of the people who run the business on the other. Success in retailing is based above all upon the understanding of people. And from the management point of view, it is based on the capacity to encourage a large and complex team

to work effectively to its full potential. It also depends upon the flair for sales and profitability that we refer to as commercial awareness.

The third reason is the company's commitment to producing high quality and, where possible, British-made merchandise. To this end it has, as already indicated, established excellent working relationships with its suppliers. The company is also at the forefront in its use of technology to improve almost every aspect of its business. This is vital for a company whose product output is in millions rather than thousands, as in the case of Next. Recent technological developments include new textile technology to produce much-improved lycra hosiery; a computerized pattern and fabric cutting process which does in two hours what used to take a pattern cutter two days; a computerized distribution network to ensure that the right products always reach the right stores on time; and an advanced information technology system which has transformed the efficiency of the company's stock control, sales forecasting, ordering and financial analysis and, as a result, made top management much better informed. Such innovations not only show that Marks and Spencer is adapting to technological change, but that it is committed to using technology to improve the quality of its products and its business.

The fourth reason is the company's ability to know what it is good at, what its customers want and, consequently, what sells. In this respect Marks and Spencer is not, and never has been, a fashion leader. It does not set out to shape innovative design trends, but rather to provide a wide range of good quality fashion classics which represent value for money, and appeal to the broadest cross-section of people possible. With such huge production runs, financial investment and vast 'customer profile', the company cannot afford to indulge in expensive 'one-off' fashion gimmicks which may last only one season and appeal to a minority of people in one geographical area. Instead, Marks and Spencer must produce a broad range of merchandise, from smart 'classic' looks to 'easy-to-wear' casual looks, within which smaller, more specific ranges can be targeted at specific stores according to their size, how much stock they can accommodate and realistically sell, local customer requirements and geographical area. For example, a small rural branch may require a small, low-cost but appealing range of warm knitwear, 'barbour' type jackets and stout footwear; whereas a large city branch may require the full range of the company's most stylish and expensive products.

It is this ability to know both its customers and its products that has been the major reason for the company's success. All four factors mentioned so far are neatly summarized in its eight basic principles:

1 To sell high quality and good-value clothing for the family, fashion for the home and a range of fine foods.

2 To create an attractive, efficient shopping environment for customers.

3 To provide a friendly, helpful service from well-trained staff.

4 To share mutually beneficial, long-term partnerships with suppliers, encouraging them to use modern and efficient production techniques.

5 To support British industry and buy abroad only when new ideas, technology, quality and value are not available in the UK.

6 To ensure staff and shareholders share in the success of the company.

7 Constantly to seek to improve quality standards in all areas of the company's operations.

8 To foster good human relations with customers, staff, suppliers and the community.

So, how does the company put these principles into practice? The 'core' of Marks and Spencer's retail operation is at its head office in Baker Street, London. From here, all the company's stores and suppliers are directed and monitored in terms of company policy, strategy, development, finance, product planning and buying, and anything else that affects the general running of the business. Such a degree of centralization requires skilled and tightly-knit teams of people who together cover a wide range of management activities, including information technology, merchandising, design forecasting, product selection and product technology, and in so doing oversee the design, manufacture, quality, distribution and marketing of all Marks and Spencer's products.

At Marks and Spencer, these teams are known as 'buying teams'. They are made up of merchandisers, selectors and technologists. Each team is responsible for a different product area, for example, men's knitwear, cosmetics or wine, and its success depends on the team's ability to work together, to make fast and accurate commercial decisions and, as a result, provide the company's customers with the right products at the right price.

The merchandisers are central to Marks and Spencer's commercial operation. They must have a complete knowledge of the market and the ability to make the correct commercial decisions. They are accountable for the profitability of Marks and Spencer's products, and their job is complex and responsible. The merchandisers' first task is to set the financial budgets for their particular product range and to assess the commercial viability of any new products in which the selectors have shown an interest. Once satisfied with the products' market appeal, the merchandiser must ensure that the supplier can meet the contract and produce the right goods at the right price, in the correct quantities and on time. Even when the contract has been signed, the merchandisers must still be completely involved with the products. They must allocate the correct quantities to specific stores and, once in the stores, monitor their sales by analysing how they are selling, where and when they are selling and if they are correctly priced.

The selector's role is to develop the right style and quality of merchandise at the right price for the Marks and Spencer customer. This requires a combination of sound commercial awareness and creative flair. The selector's first task is to work closely with the company's in-house design forecasting team to predict future fashion trends and to find out which themes, colours, fabrics, shapes and styles will be in fashion in a year's time. They visit yarn, fabric and fashion shows, read the fashion press, and monitor everything which might influence style changes. The selector and design forecaster then balance the designer's fashion ideas with the selector's knowledge of what their suppliers can produce, and what will sell, and an important directional design brief is drawn up. This outlines a basic range of products to be developed, including their colours, fabrics, shapes and styles, and forms the buying team's buying policy for the following year. This buying policy is then presented to a wide range of

appropriate suppliers whose highly commercial design and production teams, under the guidance of the selector, put it into practice
and produce the actual merchandise. From this, the selector and her
colleagues in the buying team choose those products which meet all
their requirements, and it is these that eventually find their way into
Marks and Spencer's stores.

Both merchandisers and selectors depend a great deal on their
clothing and textile technologists for technical information about a
garment or fabric so that its quality can be assessed, maintained or
improved, and for technological co-ordination with suppliers.
Marks and Spencer's technologists play a vital role in product development, and are constantly searching their specialist fields for
improvements, opportunities and major innovations. They attend
fabric, yarn and machinery fairs throughout Europe and help the
company to be a leader in technology as well as in style, quality and
value.

Marks and Spencer People and their Jobs

Designer/Forecaster

Edwina is responsible for the design of knitwear and leisurewear for
Marks and Spencer. She works with a team of designers based at the
company's head office in London.

Edwina did a degree in fashion design at Liverpool Polytechnic,
followed by a masters degree at the Royal College of Art in London.
She left college with a particular interest in knitwear design and
went to work in the forecasting studio of an Italian yarn and fibre
company. Her role was to predict which yarns, fabrics, colours and
styles would be in fashion in one or two years' time.

After six months, Edwina returned to England and worked as a
designer for several high street companies, including Stirling Cooper
and Radley. The hours were long and the pay was low but Edwina
learnt every aspect of garment production, including pattern cutting
and machining.

While working for these companies, Edwina developed her own
freelance work and began to teach in various colleges. She produced

knitwear collections for the International Wool Secretariat and several companies abroad, and freelanced full time for three years. During this period, Edwina also ran a small design studio for three days a week. There she designed a wide range of garments, including knitwear, and increased her managerial experience.

Through a colleague, who had seen her work at a Young Designers Exhibition at Olympia in London, Edwina was then invited to work for Daniel Hechter in Paris. This gave her a wonderful opportunity to develop her own ideas while, at the same time, being given the exciting opportunity to design the entire range of Daniel Hechter knitwear. Edwina also enjoyed the less commercial constraints of designing the company's twice-yearly fashion show for the press. After four years, Edwina returned to London to work for Alexon, a very different company from Daniel Hechter. Alexon's clothing was aimed at a more formal and, in many ways, limited market, but two years' experience with them gave Edwina an excellent introduction to working for an English design company once again.

From Alexon, Edwina joined the Conran Design Group, and for a short time designed merchandise for Richard Shops. She then joined Sabre, a leading men's knitwear company, and was asked to design a completely new range of women's knitwear and related jersey separates. Edwina worked closely with the production team in the company's own factory, and became involved with many technical as well as creative decisions. Frustrated by the increasing limitations of her role, Edwina left Sabre to teach on the fashion design course at Kingston Polytechnic, and found it fascinating to be involved with young designers at the outset of their careers. Most recently, Edwina was invited to join Marks and Spencer's design team. Edwina accepted, delighted and intrigued by the idea of joining a 'forecasting' studio and liaising with buying departments.

Edwina predicts future fashion trends and initiates new ideas to be developed by the company's knitwear and leisurewear departments, and by their suppliers. At the beginning of each season, Edwina and her senior selector visit yarn, fabric and fashion shows to find out which styles, colours, themes, shapes and fabrics will be in fashion in a year's time. On their return, Edwina adapts and develops her findings to suit the requirements of Marks and Spencer and its customers. Her ideas and drawings are presented to the senior selector and together they devise a 'departmental design brief'. This forms the basis on which the following year's leisurewear and knitwear is designed and produced. More detailed versions of the brief are then presented to the suppliers and their design teams, and Edwina works closely with them to put her ideas into production.

Edwina's role is not suitable for a young, inexperienced designer. It requires sound commercial knowledge, equal to that of the senior selectors, and good judgement and communication skills to guide and inspire a wide range of suppliers and their design and production teams.

Edwina's advice to young designers is to gain a wide range of design knowledge and industrial experience, to be confident and to use their initiative.

Design Pattern Cutter

Peter is the senior design pattern cutter in Marks and Spencer's in-house design studio in London. He heads a small team of four skilled technicians who work closely with the designers. The technicians interpret the designers' ideas, cut patterns from their sketches, make the first 'toiles' (prototype garments), cut the fabric and supervise the making of the original sample garments. They then assess the finished samples with the designers to ensure that the required standard of excellence has been achieved.

On leaving school, Peter was apprenticed to a small tailoring business in the East End of London. He began at a junior level, cutting out linings for coats and jackets, but gradually progressed to pattern cutting. This inspired Peter to find out more about garment design in general, and he moved on to work for several well-known freelance designers, including Bill Gibb. For nine years Peter worked with Bill Gibb's senior pattern cutter. There, Peter not only learnt about every aspect of garment construction, including block making, toile making and sample making, but also about the more creative facets of fashion design, including style, shape, colour and texture. Although the work was exciting and introduced Peter to the world of top fashion design, his career progression was limited. With a young family to support, Peter decided to move on to a large and well-established company. He joined Marks and Spencer as a design pattern cutter and gradually progressed to his present role.

Peter and his small team offer an invaluable support and technical advisory service to Marks and Spencer via the in-house design team. Peter's association with the design team begins each season when he accompanies them to international fabric and fashion fairs. There he observes the latest fashion trends in order to understand what the design team may require from him in the next few months. On his return, Peter helps the design team to prepare their findings for a major presentation to the selectors and suppliers. This presentation consists of a forecast, a year in advance, of the major future fashion trends. Prior to the presentation, Peter and his team work from the designer's ideas and sketches to produce patterns. From these, they make first a toile and then a finished sample garment. The toile is tried on, enabling the designer to see if his or her ideas turn into a wearable garment, and then adapted and refined until it fits perfectly. The sample garment shows exactly what the finished garment will look like and enables the designer to communicate his or her ideas clearly at the presentation. After the presentation, Peter and his team work with the designers and selectors to produce some of the key new shapes and styles of garments to guide the manufacturers and suppliers during the initial stages of production.

Peter works with the technical services department continually to assess and improve these key new shapes. Each type of Marks and Spencer garment – for example, a ladies' tie-neck blouse or man's short-sleeved shirt – is based on a standard 'pattern block'. These blocks are devised by the technicians to help the manufacturers to produce accurate shapes, styles and sizes of garment. Peter must check that, although made from standard patterns, the garments still retain style, flair and individuality.

When recruiting new staff, Peter looks for candidates with a sound technical training and a flair for design. He stresses that a designer and pattern cutter are a team, and that pattern cutting can be as creative and exciting as designing.

Senior Selector

Margaret is the senior selector for Marks and Spencer's ladies' leisurewear. She is based at the company's head office in London.

Margaret did a degree in business studies. This introduced her to all facets of business, including law and accountancy, management, communication and organizational skills, and gave her a sound basis from which to move into any area of business or commerce.

On graduating, Margaret joined Marks and Spencer as a graduate trainee in store management. A six-month induction course introduced her to every aspect of the company, after which Margaret was made a departmental manager in a large Marks and Spencer store. This taught her directly about the company's market, its merchandise and its customers. It also gave Margaret an insight into her colleagues' roles and she decided to retrain as a selector. Margaret was attached to a senior selector and then placed in those departments with which she would eventually work, including design, merchandising and quality control. This not only helped Margaret to understand the principles and procedures of buying merchandise, but also made her realize she would be part of a large team.

After six months, Margaret became an assistant selector in several departments and then a range selector for ladies' accessories. This gave her an exciting opportunity to source and develop a new range of merchandise, and increased her experience of dealing with all kinds of suppliers and manufacturers. Through hard work and initiative, Margaret was promoted to a senior selector, first for ladies' knitwear and more recently for ladies' leisurewear, her current position.

Margaret is responsible for all the product development within the ladies' leisurewear department. Together with her team of assistant selectors and range selectors, she must develop the right style and quality of merchandise at the right price for the Marks and Spencer customer. To this end, Margaret constantly visits fashion and trade shows, reads the fashion press, monitors competitors, meets her suppliers and manufacturers, and stays in close contact with the design, merchandising and quality control departments at head office.

Margaret's contact with the design studio begins each season when the designers present the senior selectors from each department and their suppliers with a 'storyboard'. This outlines, in drawings, photographs and fabric swatches, the main fashion themes for a year ahead, including the colours, shapes, styles and fabrics. Each selector is then assigned to the relevant designer and together they draw up a 'departmental brief'. They balance the designer's fashion ideas with Margaret's knowledge of what her suppliers can produce and what will sell, and outline a basic range of garments to be developed. This might include, for example, three styles of jogging tops and trousers, four styles of shirts and six styles of jerseys all in three main colour themes. This brief is crucial because it forms the basis on which the following year's range of leisurewear is developed and produced, and forms the buying policy for Margaret's department.

In addition to the departmental brief, Margaret and the designer must also devise more specific versions of it for each of the leisurewear suppliers and their design teams. Although Marks and Spencer's design team has established the basic fashion direction, it is now the suppliers' designers who must put the suggestions into practice. Guided by Margaret's commercial knowledge, they develop an initial range of sample garments known as 'buying samples'. At a series of 'work-in-progress' presentations at head office, Margaret and her selectors, the merchandisers and quality controllers choose those buying samples which, in their opinion, should be developed for full production. During the development work, Margaret keeps in close contact with the suppliers, advising on any technical problems and ensuring that they produce merchandise of quality at a price which will sell.

Margaret also works closely with the merchandising and quality control departments. She helps the merchandisers to allocate their budgets across garment ranges by advising them, from a fashion and customer viewpoint, on what will sell best and at what price. This prevents the merchandisers from relying solely on past sales figures to predict what will or will not sell. A change in fashion trends and seasonal weather might suggest, for example, that although mini-skirts were a best-seller last season, they will look outdated this season.

Margaret's contact with the quality controllers is to ensure that her suppliers produce merchandise which meets Marks and Spencer's high standards of quality. To this end, she will work with the company's fabric and garment technologists and the suppliers' production teams to improve, for example, the quality of a fabric, the fit of a garment or the efficiency of a whole production process.

Margaret's job is responsible and demanding. She must constantly pull together the experience and expertise of everyone involved in the development of new merchandise, and objectively balance their ideas and requirements with what the customer really wants. This needs excellent judgement, confidence and an ability to communicate with all kinds of people.

When appointing trainee selectors, Margaret recruits from four main sources – from existing Marks and Spencer employees who want to become selectors; from college graduates with a business or design background, or who have already done an industrial placement with the company; and from experienced personnel from other areas of the fashion industry. The successful candidates must have initiative, combine creative flair with commercial awareness, be confident, organized and well-presented.

Knitwear Designer

Gina is the senior knitwear designer for one of Marks and Spencer's major suppliers. She works in the supplier's own design studio in Leicestershire, and frequently visits Marks and Spencer's head office in London.

Gina did a degree in textile design at Leeds University. The course gave her a broad background in printed, woven and knitted textiles, and was much more technically and commercially orientated than many other courses.

On leaving university, Gina worked for Jaeger, where she received a good training in upmarket knitwear design, garment construction and yarn sourcing, but gained very little commercial experience. This was soon put right at Gina Fiori, a supplier of knitwear to leading high street stores, including Marks and Spencer. Gina now had to design to specific price points, and for a wide and very varied market. At this stage, Gina decided that she would like to work for a larger Marks and Spencer supplier, and joined the Paisley-Hyper Group, a dynamic company with a young and design-conscious management team. Although the company has no specific house-style, it specializes in technological innovations with yarn dyers and finishers – for example, printed knitwear – sourcing new and unusual yarns, and adapting Italian knitwear trends to the British market.

Gina heads a team of designers and make-up staff, including several ladieswear and menswear designers who, together with a yarn and garment technologist and a technical manager, form the design/development team.

Gina's role begins when she and her design team visit the European yarn and fabric prediction shows. There they source exciting new yarns suitable for next year's knitwear collections; buy yarn and knitted fabric samples in which Marks and Spencer are already interested, and discuss possible ideas with relevant yarn and fabric suppliers.

On their return, Gina and her team collate all their information and put together a small collection of yarns suitable for mens- and womenswear. In a Spring/Summer season this might include cotton, cotton and acrylic, acrylic and linen yarns, suitable for a variety of garments at a variety of prices.

Gina and her colleagues then attend a major presentation at Marks and Spencer's head office. Together with all the main knitwear suppliers, they are given the general 'directional' brief by Marks and Spencer's own design forecasting team. This outlines the main fashion themes, shapes, styles and colours of knitwear required by Marks and Spencer for the year ahead. Gina is then briefed in more detail by a selector, according to what she needs to make up the knitwear ranges, and what Gina's company does best. This might be to develop a range of jacquard designs, or a collection of 'classic' cotton knitwear.

A few weeks later, Gina presents her yarn collection and initial drawings of her new knitwear to the selector who decides which of them should be developed. Gina and her technical team then turn the yarns into knitted fabrics and work the fabrics into sample garments. The selector suggests how they might be improved, and exactly how much they should cost. Gina carries out the suggestions and, at a final selection meeting, presents perfect sample garments at the correct price to the senior knitwear selector. She decides which of them should go into production and orders are placed with Gina's company.

Throughout the development of a new range of knitwear, Gina constantly liaises with Marks and Spencer's selectors, and with every member of her team. This ensures that she achieves the best results at the best price. The yarn technologist helps Gina to source new yarns and test their quality; the garment technologist 'grades' the sample garments into different sizes, and the technical manager solves any foreseeable production problems. He develops new production processes to raise standards or lower costs; solves problems of, for example, weak stitching; advises on whether a new knitted fabric can be produced in huge quantities and still retain its quality, and so on.

Gina's designers are practical and commercial, helping her to produce high quality knitwear at competitive prices. Gina sums up their joint role:

> A successful design team is one which can design to a specific price point, for example, £14.99 or £19.99, and still give the customer that little something extra; a team which can interpret the latest 'looks', colours and shapes for a mass market.

Fashion Press Officer

Gillian is a fashion press officer for Marks and Spencer. She is responsible for promoting ladieswear and lingerie. Gillian has a varied background in journalism and public relations and has brought new ideas and contacts to the company.

On leaving school, Gillian worked as an editorial assistant on a sports magazine. She had always been interested in fashion and often featured articles on fashionable sportswear. From the sports magazine, Gillian moved on to become a press officer at British Home Stores. There she received a good training in publicity and promotion, and began to build up a list of useful contacts, something vital for a press officer. Gillian then worked for a variety of large fashion and retail companies. At this stage, Gillian decided that she needed to widen her experience so she joined an independent public relations agency. The agency dealt with a wide range of different clients, including homeware and furniture companies, babywear manufacturers, food retailers, and so on. This gave Gillian the broad background she required and she joined Marks and Spencer as a valuable and capable press officer.

Gillian's basic role is to protect and promote Marks and Spencer, its image and its merchandise. She must ensure that any information given to the public, either directly or through the media, is correct and an accurate reflection of company policy.

At the beginning of each season, Gillian organizes a publicity programme to promote the latest ranges of ladieswear and lingerie to the public. This includes special events such as fashion shows, press releases and nationwide publicity in the media.

The first stage of the programme is to promote the new ranges to the national newspapers and magazines. Using her extensive list of contacts and knowledge of journalism, Gillian targets collections of garments from the new ranges at specific journalists and their publications. She might target a range of practical anoraks at a journalist on an outdoor pursuits magazine; or a set of silk lingerie at the fashion editor of a glossy woman's magazine. The journalists are then invited to borrow the garments, and style, photograph and write about them in a manner appropriate to their readers.

The second stage of the programme is to promote the new ranges in the regional newspapers. Gillian reviews all the garments and, guided by the image that Marks and Spencer wish to convey, current fashion trends, and the interests of the journalists, selects those garments which, from her experience, will make newsworthy 'stories'. She might choose garments which follow a fashionable theme – the nautical or 'classic' look; highlight a stylish colour combination, or feature a popular fabric – suede or denim. Gillian then produces a press release about the garments and a set of photographs with 'copy' to illustrate her 'story'. To ensure that the pictures convey the right image, Gillian chooses the most appropriate models and locations; directs the photographer and styles the clothes (puts them together and adds relevant accessories). This is one of the more creative aspects of Gillian's job and requires individual flair and good visual judgement. Once the package is complete, it is sent to all the regional papers. Their fashion journalists can use it as it stands or as part of their own fashion 'story'.

The world of public relations is small. Gillian's role requires a huge range of contacts, from journalists to model agencies, and a great deal of credibility. Both are gained only with experience. When recruiting new fashion press officers, Marks and Spencer tends to choose existing in-house personnel who know about the company, or occasionally outside candidates with wide PR experience. Such candidates are expected to be well presented, articulate and enthusiastic about their company and the fashion industry.

5 Paul Smith Ltd

Paul Smith Ltd is a leading and self-financed menswear company which designs and sells a wide range of unusual and upmarket men's clothing, accessories and stylish 'ephemeral merchandise'. This ephemeral merchandise includes pens, watches, glassware, cuff-links, jewellery, mirrors, radios, antique or collectable toys, trinkets and books, *objets d'art* and modern furniture and sculpture. Much of the furniture and sculpture is commissioned from young British designers and makers.

Over the last ten years, Paul Smith Ltd has gradually been built up from a small menswear shop in Nottingham to a highly successful international business with additional shops in London, Japan and New York. The company has also developed a thriving wholesale business directed from Nottingham. This now forms the backbone of the company and supplies upmarket department stores and designer shops throughout the world with Paul Smith merchandise.

In addition to achieving financial success in a difficult and ever-changing industry, Paul Smith Ltd has had a far-reaching influence over men's fashion, especially in Britain. It has raised the average British male's level of fashion consciousness and caused many high street shops and department stores to re-think their approach to menswear. Thanks to Paul Smith Ltd, many British men have been persuaded out of their ill-fitting suits, plain shirts and drab ties and into well-cut, colourful jackets, decorative shirts and crazy ties. Even well-established chain stores are following in the company's shoes. For example, in 1980, Paul Smith Ltd was the first company to revive men's boxer shorts, re-vamping them in bright colours and eccentric fabric designs. Today Marks and Spencer does an excellent trade in this line of merchandise.

But such success and influence is not achieved quickly or easily. Paul Smith Ltd, like Marks and Spencer, comes from very ordinary beginnings.

Paul Smith left school in Nottingham when he was fifteen years old. He had always been interested in clothes and fashion, and spent several years working in local clothes shops as a sales assistant, and for manufacturers as a general dogsbody to learn all he could about the fashion industry. In 1968 he met Pauline Denyer, a fashion design lecturer and graduate ot the Royal College of Art in London. Two years later, Denyer persuaded Smith to open his own menswear shop from tiny premises in a back street of Nottingham. The two could only afford to open the shop on Fridays and Saturdays. Smith spent the rest of the week searching for new stock, choosing only clothes that he would wear himself. As the need to earn money to buy new stock increased, Smith began to do a wide range of fashion consultancy work, gradually building up an impressive list of clients, including the International Wool Secretariat and Browns, the upmarket London clothier. This not only boosted Smith's income, but also gave him a great deal of commercial experience and many invaluable business contacts.

One of these contacts, a Northern clothing manufacturer, called Smith in to update and rescue its flagging business. Within an afternoon he was made its managing director, and in only six months had earned enough money to be able to set up his own design and wholesale business. Under the experienced guidance of Pauline Denyer, Smith learnt every aspect of fashion design and production, including how to source fabrics, pattern making and cutting, garment construction and tailoring. Having persuaded old-fashioned fabric mills and traditional menswear manufacturers to have faith in his imaginative and unusual designs, Smith produced his first range of men's shirts. Fortunately, this sold immediately to a forward-looking New York store and Paul Smith was launched on an, as yet, unsuspecting market! Smith and Denyer slowly and carefully developed a range of trousers and jackets, evolving, as they went along, the now unmistakable Paul Smith style.

With increased success, Smith realized that, although his Nottingham shop was now open full time and the main showcase for his clothing, he urgently needed a London outlet to put him on the fashion map.

At first, Smith looked in all the obvious places but, inspired by what had happened to old warehouses and market halls in Paris, Barcelona and New York, chose to set up shop in Covent Garden well before it was chic and fashionable. Helped by a sculptor friend, Peter Wigglesworth, Smith transformed an almost derelict building in Floral Street into a shop with showrooms for his new collections and offices for his wholesale business. Paul Smith had arrived. Over the next decade, Paul Smith and his then small team of employees worked long and hard, painstakingly building up the retail and wholesale business, Paul Smith Ltd, to its present level.

Like Next and Marks and Spencer, the secret of the eventual success of Paul Smith Ltd lies in the nature of its products, the people who create and manufacture those products, and the company's attitude towards its customers. In the case of Paul Smith Ltd, one person in particular has influenced, and continues to influence, the success of the business – Paul Smith himself. He is not only the managing director of the company, but also the designer of its clothes and shops, the selector of its accessories and ephemeral merchandise, and the driving force behind its wholesale operation. In short, the company is founded on Paul Smith's own inspired and highly subjective vision. This places it in a unique position in the fashion industry. It not only ensures that Paul Smith is continually involved in all facets of his business, but also that he retains a personal and individual touch that many other companies of a similar size and nature cannot. In an era when so many high street stores are beginning to look the same, this is unusual and refreshing.

So what kind of effect does Paul Smith's influence have on his business? The first major effect is on the nature of the products that the company sells. All the merchandise, from the clothing to the Coronation mugs, Dinky toys, toy robots and first edition books collected on his travels, has the distinctive and eclectic Paul Smith style. This style is best shown in his clothing. Paul Smith delights in taking elements of the classic English Gentleman's style, and adding to them a quirky, humorous or surprising twist. This might be in the detailing, cut, colour or choice of fabric of a garment, or the way in which that garment is unexpectedly combined with another. For example, a classic English blazer might be combined with a crazy spotted, striped or patterned tie, a smart striped shirt might be worn with humorous rabbit-shaped cuff-links, or a traditional 'city' suit might be made from permanently creased linen and worn with brightly coloured socks:

Paul Smith clothes allow you to be yourself. They're often

> classic but have interesting colours and fabrics. My things are deliberately mismatched, and they've got a strong sense of humour.

Whatever the quirky twist or whacky humour, Paul Smith's clothes are always well made either in Britain or Italy and from the best quality fabrics – a further result of his strong personal influence. Smith himself constantly seeks out new and exciting fabric suppliers throughout the world and this is something for which he and his company have become renowned:

> The speciality of the house is the cloth which is the best, the finest in the world.

The second major effect of Paul Smith's influence is on the invaluable, close-knit and adaptable team of people who, under his guidance, either help to design, make or source his merchandise; or who help to run his highly successful retail and wholesale business. This team has been carefully built up over the years and, although it has increased in size to twenty-five, is still relatively small when compared to both Next and Marks and Spencer. The core of Paul Smith's buying, design and production team is based in both Nottingham and London. In London it includes a buyer who helps to source the ephemeral merchandise and *objets d'art*; a young designer who helps to design the Paul Smith range of sportswear aimed at the American market, and a wholesale sales manager.

In Nottingham, the team includes an experienced assistant designer who helps Smith to transform his ideas into garments; production and accounts managers; and two of Smith's fellow directors who concentrate on the financial and day-to-day running of the company. So, how does this core design and development team operate, and how do they create and sell the distinctive Paul Smith merchandise? At the beginning of each season, Paul Smith travels throughout Britain and Europe to source unusual fabrics and to find clothing manufacturers who are willing and able to try out innovative production techniques. On his return, he and his assistant designer produce ideas and sketches for the next Paul Smith collection. The ideas and sketches are then developed into prototype garments made from calico. These enable the two designers to ensure that their ideas are feasible, and to make any necessary alterations to the garments' design and construction. Once the prototypes are ready, each one, together with its pattern, specifications and sample fabric is given to a suitable manufacturer. The manufacturer is carefully selected according to his specific production capabilities and the design team's design requirements. The manufacturer makes up a second prototype garment in the correct cloth, and the in-house production team at Paul Smith use it to work out how much the finished garment will cost. The manufacturer's own production department is also advised on any modifications which need to be made before the next stage of the process. The manufacturer then produces a small quantity of perfect garments in the correct fabric and trimmings. These 'sales samples' are subjected to a series of rigorous quality-control tests, including cloth testing, wear testing and wash testing; and carefully assessed by Paul Smith, his assistant designer and production manager. The team not only finalize the selling price of each sales sample, but also discuss its overall commercial appeal; the suitability of the cloth for each sample's particular style; whether that colour or print of cloth is available in the necessary quantities, and so on. Bearing all these factors in mind, a decision is finally taken on which sales samples to include in the new collection. Once the collection of samples is ready, it is shown at Paul Smith Ltd's own Paris fashion show, and at selling shows in Paris, New York and London, by a small team of company staff. Before each show, Paul Smith meets the fashion press and potential buyers to explain the ideas and inspiration behind the new collection. Each show lasts only a few days. During it, all the wholesale orders for the following six-month season, including those for the Paul Smith shops, are taken. For this reason, such shows are crucial to the success of the company and take months of meticulous planning by Paul Smith and his core design and production team.

Details of the wholesale orders are returned to the company's Nottingham offices and quickly and carefully analysed. From this analysis, the provisional fabric orders are confirmed and advance production schedules finalized. The production team now has only sixteen weeks in which to meet the orders. This leaves little margin for error. Every aspect of the production process is constantly monitored so that problems can be solved immediately and efficiently. Fabrics are imported, documented and quality tested, and the factories in which the garments are made are regularly visited to ensure that high production standards and reliable schedules are maintained.

Once the garments have been manufactured, they are received into the company's warehouse, thoroughly checked again, and individually sorted and packed ready to be distributed to shops and stores throughout the world. Special care is taken to observe complicated export regulations which not only vary from country to country, but also from shop to shop. After the goods' arrival in the shops and stores, Paul Smith and his team monitor sales and consumer reaction to the new range by regularly contacting their wholesale customers, including the managers of the Paul Smith shops, for feedback. Both existing and potential clients throughout the world are then visited on a country-to-country basis in order to continue and develop the personal relationship established with them at the selling shows.

In only six months the design and production process has come full circle. Paul Smith and his team of people must now begin to create and produce next year's stylish and distinctive range of Paul Smith merchandise, thus beginning the whole process again.

The third main area of Smith's influence and reason for his success is the nature of his shops themselves. Again inspired by Smith, his shops echo the same whimsical and eclectic English Gentleman style of his clothes. Each has a welcoming, almost 'old colonial' atmosphere created from a mixture of original nineteenth-century mahogany shop fittings, oil-paintings in heavy, ornate frames and highly polished wooden floors scattered with Oriental rugs. However, in typical Smith style this is suddenly upset by a crazy piece of modern sculpture or furniture. Such an atmosphere makes a refreshing change from the increasing uniformity of so many high street fashion stores with their harsh lighting, chrome fittings and noisy video screens:

> Because the whole way of shopping has tended to become so impersonal, I want people to feel that my stores are loved and that there really is someone called Paul Smith, the name above the door. I want people to enjoy coming in . . . !

To this end, Smith's shop-floor staff, whether in London, New York or Tokyo, are encouraged to help and take care of his customers, and not to persuade them to buy something they do not want or which does not suit them. This concern arises from Smith's own experience of serving in a shop and his love of selling, not just designing, clothes.

This raises the final and perhaps most important result of Smith's influence – that on his customers, without whom he would not have such a successful business. Not surprisingly, many of Smith's customers are imaginative and creative people like himself. They include fellow designers, actors, architects, painters, film directors and pop stars. Unlike Next and Marks and Spencer, Smith has not set out to appeal to a huge, popular market. However, in producing high quality and unusual clothing in an age of mass-production, Smith is inevitably enticing an ever-widening range of customers to wear his clothes, from teenagers searching for novelty socks or boxer shorts, to fashion-conscious women wanting well-cut shirts.

Paul Smith People and their Jobs

Menswear Designer

Derek Morten is Paul Smith's assistant designer. He works from a large warehouse in Nottingham, the production headquarters of the company's wholesale business.

Derek followed a course in fashion design at Derby College of Art. The course taught him the technical aspects of fashion designing, including pattern making, toile making, cloth cutting and garment construction. He then moved on to specialize in menswear design at the Royal College of Art in London. On leaving college, Derek worked for a wide variety of menswear companies and gradually built up enough industrial experience and contacts to establish his own freelance business. His menswear collections sold throughout Europe and America. However, the constant pressures of running a freelance business almost single-handed, from designing, making and selling collections and meeting orders and deadlines, to coping with inflexible British manufacturers and ever-increasing administrative work, eventually led Derek to discontinue his business. He joined Fiorucci in Italy, welcoming the opportunity to concentrate solely on his creative design work, and to liaise with innovative and adventurous fabric and clothing manufacturers – an opportunity rarely experienced in Britain.

After working for several more leading Italian and French fashion companies, Derek was invited by Paul Smith to return to Britain to become his design assistant. Paul Smith would source and buy the fabrics and Derek would liaise with manufacturers and help with the design work.

Derek has worked closely with Paul Smith since 1982. They are not overly influenced by short-lived 'high fashion' trends, but instead use their strong design sense and knowledge of customer requirements to guide their work. A small team of co-operative and versatile assistants also dovetail to do whatever is required. This might include helping to make up prototype garments, supervising fabric trims, writing sample orders, co-ordinating new fabric samples, dispatching fabric lengths to manufacturers, organizing fabric shipment dates, and so on. Derek stresses that such versatility is vital in a small design team. A young designer must be prepared to turn his or her hand to anything.

Derek's main role starts at the beginning of each season when Paul Smith returns from his travels having sourced unusual fabrics and found innovative manufacturers throughout Britain and Europe. Derek then works closely with Paul Smith to develop his findings into ideas and sketches for the next Paul Smith collection. The ideas might be inspired by a particular colour or type of fabric that Paul Smith has found, or by a new manufacturing process which makes possible the production of more complex or imaginative garment designs. Derek and his small team of assistants then develop the ideas into prototype garments made from calico. These enable the two designers to ensure that their ideas can be transformed into wearable garments, and to make any necessary alterations to their design and construction. Once the prototype garments are ready, each one, together with its pattern, specifications and sample fabric, is given to a suitable manufacturer. It is Derek's responsibility to select the most appropriate manufacturer according to that manufacturer's specific production capabilities and Derek's design requirements. The manufacturer makes up a second prototype garment in the correct cloth, and the production team at Paul Smith Ltd uses it to work out how much the finished garment will cost. Derek also advises the manufacturer's production department on any modifications which need to be made before the next stage of the process.

The manufacturer then produces a small quantity of perfect garments in the correct fabrics and trimmings. After being subjected to a series of strict quality-control procedures, these sales samples are carefully reviewed by Paul Smith, Derek and the production manager. Together they assess every aspect of the sales samples, including their overall commercial appeal, their final selling price, the suitability of the fabric for each garment's style, the availability of that fabric, and so on. After much detailed discussion, a decision is finally reached on which of the sales samples to include in the new collection.

Once the collection of samples is ready to be shown in Paul Smith's Paris fashion show, and in selling shows in Paris, London and New York, Derek's main responsibilities are largely over. Although he will obviously monitor the progress of the new collection and consumer reaction to it, Derek is now free to begin to plan next year's Paul Smith collections. His colleagues in the production and wholesale departments, under Paul Smith's guidance, now take responsibility for selling the collection, meeting orders and distributing it throughout the world.

Derek Morten enjoys working with such a creative and enthusiastic team. His advice to young designers starting out is to work hard, be extremely businesslike and, above all, versatile. He stresses that, in a complex and ever-changing industry, it is vital to be aware of every aspect of the fashion business, in particular manufacturing and wholesaling. A young designer in Britain must be able to liaise with a wide variety of manufacturers in order to put his or her ideas into practice, and should be prepared to do any job within the industry in order to gain experience.

Shop Manager

Amanda manages the Paul Smith shop in Nottingham, Paul Smith's home town.

On leaving school, Amanda had a variety of jobs, including working as a nanny and helping to run a stall in Kensington market. She was always interested in fashion and, quite by accident through a friend, was invited to become the personal assistant to a well-known fashion designer who was then just starting out. Amanda did all kinds of things, from stock-taking and book-keeping to helping to prepare the designer's collections for fashion shows and trade exhibitions. Although the work was varied and gave Amanda an insight into the world of high fashion, it was demanding and frequently poorly paid. Disillusioned, Amanda decided to leave London and move to Nottingham. A friend at Paul Smith's London shop suggested she apply for a sales assistant's job in the Nottingham branch.

Amanda followed his advice and gradually worked her way up from shop assistant to shop manageress, her present role. Amanda is responsible for many aspects of the shop, including its day-to-day running, its stock and the management of its staff.

At the beginning of each season, Amanda visits Paul Smith's London showroom to look at his latest collection of sample garments and accessories. Based on a knowledge of her customers' specific requirements, past sales figures and her own taste, Amanda selects and orders a range of garments suitable for the Nottingham shop. Although she has freedom of choice, the distinctive Paul Smith style is always maintained because it is so strong and quirky.

Once the new collection arrives, each garment is pressed, brushed, priced and carefully displayed in the shop. Guided by the seasonal looks shown in videos and photographs of the whole collection taken at the Paul Smith fashion show in Paris, Amanda co-ordinates the garments. She does this in ways which not only illustrate how the clothes should be worn, but which will also appeal to her many and varied regular customers, and to the fashion stylists who frequently hire the garments for photographic shoots.

On a more daily basis, Amanda ensures that the shop, its stock and her staff always look their best; that customers are treated courteously; that problems are solved as quickly and efficiently as possible; that stock is counted and reordered on time; that sales figures are carefully recorded; and that weekly takings are accurately calculated. Such responsibilities require energy, and total commitment to Paul Smith Ltd, its merchandise, its shop and its customers. In return, Amanda enjoys a high degree of managerial freedom and the opportunity to run the only designer fashion shop in the city.

Part 3   Ways of Working

There are three main ways of working in fashion – through design consultancies, companies or freelancing. In this part we meet a variety of people who epitomize the extraordinary range of the fashion industry and the significance of design within it. Reading these stories should help you to get a feel of the aspect of the industry that appeals to you and to decide the role you might like to play in the future.

6 Design Consultancies

Fashion and Colour Consultant

Sue Ryder Richardson is a freelance fashion and colour consultant. Her training had nothing to do with fashion design. She studied English literature and art history at university, intending to become an art gallery curator. Instead, Sue worked in art publishing for two years and, quite unexpectedly through a friend, joined the public relations and marketing department of I. M. International. After three years, I. M. International moved to New York and Sue was asked to start their British centre and work freelance as their public relations and marketing consultant. I. M. International was an advance fashion trend and colour information service supplying clothing manufacturers and retailers throughout the world. Sue did public relations work with the company's existing clients, found new clients, gave colour presentations and developed design concepts introduced in the company's monthly subscription magazines. In 1988, I. M. International ceased trading. Sue set up her own advance fashion trend and colour information service, tailoring it to the exact needs and pockets of her clients, and using the many contacts made at I. M. International.

The colour information on which Sue bases her service is produced eighteen to twenty months ahead of season. The colour palette is restricted to approximately thirty colours and these are divided into 'trend moods': a pale theme, a neutral theme, some bright and some dark colours. Depending on the season and the current fashion trends, emphasis will be on particular colour ranges. For example, in Autumn 1988, reds, greens, purples and burgundies predominated. These colours are discussed almost two years ahead of season at a large meeting in Paris. This is attended by colour consultants and large organizations including the International Wool Secretariat. The colour ranges are agreed and each consultant or company adapts them for their own use. Wool companies work on wool colours, cotton on cotton, and colour consultants look at colours in terms of trends or fashions for future seasons.

Sue's role is then to send this information out to her clients eighteen months before they need it. She also looks at designer collections to see how the colours have been used and to spot any exciting new looks which can also be passed on to her clients in constant updates.

Sue's advice to someone starting out in this area is to do a degree in fashion and textile design, including a work placement with either a fashion consultancy group, or in the design studio of a major fabric manufacturer. All fabric design work is done well ahead of the actual fashion season so ideas and trends are at their newest and freshest in a fabric design studio. On leaving college, Sue advises students to work for a reputable fashion information company before setting up on their own. As few manufacturers and retailers have in-house colour consultants, most work freelance. This requires sound financial advice, self-discipline, determination and hard work.

Fashion Design Forecaster

Joy Elphick is the chief administrator of Design Intelligence Limited, a fashion design forecasting company based in Covent Garden, London.

Joy did a diploma in business studies followed by various jobs in personnel management, modelling and fashion journalism. She then joined a large retail organization and took responsibility for the design division which gradually developed into Design Intelligence Limited. Although Joy had no formal training in fashion design, her mixed work experience and strong personal interest in design gave her the attributes to do her present job. This includes administration, production schedules, personnel management, handling company accounts and liaising with agents throughout the world.

Design Intelligence Limited supplies fashion design forecast information to designers, buyers and merchandisers in large retail stores, textile and clothing manufacturers, and freelance fashion designers. It covers colour, fabric and styling information for womenswear, menswear, childrenswear and knitwear, and this is released to the clients sixteen months ahead of the actual fashion season. The information is supplied in high quality colour, trend and style books produced by the company's in-house graphic design team. Hundreds of design ideas and information sources are presented in detailed and accurate fashion drawings, colour palettes and real fabric swatches. The client can then use this information in whatever way he likes, confident that he is now aware of the latest colours and fabrics, and the most stylish fashion designs. In addition, he can always telephone or visit the company's studios to get further advice.

All this information is the result of extensive research by the company's in-house team of fashion designers. Together they visit fashion shows and exhibitions, attend colour presentations, watch influential films and theatre, observe trends in graphics, interior design and architecture, and monitor the general economic and social climate to find out which trends and ideas will influence fashion design in future seasons. The designers then sift their findings and begin to put together their colour, fabric and style forecasts. Throughout, they liaise with fabric dyers and manufacturers to ensure that the predicted colours and fabrics really will exist by the actual fashion season.

Every designer at Design Intelligence Limited has a degree in fashion and textile design from a leading art college. Designers have to work quickly and under great pressure, and must accept that their ideas will not materialize until they are put into production by one of the company's clients. This can be frustrating and disappointing, especially if the final garments are very different from the original ideas.

Joy Elphick's advice to someone starting out in this area is to study fashion and textile design at art college, to gain industrial and commercial experience in a large retail company or textile/clothing manufacturer, and to work extremely hard.

Design Consultant

Anne Tyrrell is a leading fashion and textile design consultant, and a part-time lecturer/senior tutor in the school of fashion at the Royal College of Art, London.

Anne did courses in fashion design at Norwich School of Art and the Royal College of Art. On leaving college she found it difficult to find a design job because 'design' did not yet enjoy the high profile it does today, and because she had little industrial experience. For two years, Anne worked in a basement as a pattern cutter and grader. She hated it but gained invaluable technical experience. Anne then joined a fellow ex-RCA student as a design assistant. She cut his patterns, made toiles, supervised production schedules and visited factories to oversee the manufacture of his garments. She also began to lecture at several art colleges and became very committed to design education.

Unexpectedly, Anne was invited to join John Marks, a leading clothing manufacturer. She set up a design room, designed collections, made patterns, cut fabric, supervised production – in short, did everything from origination of ideas to garment manufacture. Gradually, John Marks developed into an international company and Anne was given her own label and design team. She was also made a director of the company. She now produced day wear, evening wear and separates, showed at all the international fashion fairs and sold her collections to major stores throughout the world.

In 1983, Anne's co-director decided to retire and after twenty years Anne decided that it was time to try something new. With a small portfolio of clients, a studio, a telephone, pattern cutter and sample machinist, Anne set up Anne Tyrrell Design, her own design consultancy. The consultancy has now expanded to include seven in-house designers from the Royal College of Art and other leading art schools, pattern cutters and sample machinists. Together they cover areas of design in menswear, womenswear, childrenswear, knitwear, printed textiles, lingerie, sportswear, corporate uniforms, colour forecasting, fabric sourcing, dyeing and buying, pattern cutting, toile and sample making and production management. This enables the team to offer each client a complete custom-made package to meet his exact requirements. If additional help is required, Anne uses her network of freelance designers, made up mostly of her own ex-students. The consultancy now has clients throughout Europe, America and the Far East, and Anne's aim is to take on even more diverse and exciting projects.

Her advice to someone starting out is to be dedicated and organized; to be versatile and prepared to work as a responsible member of a team; to soak up information and inspiration; and to gain as much creative, technical and managerial experience as possible.

7 Companies

Textile Designers

Christine Langley and Shirley Lineker form Circus, a small company specializing in hand-printed designer clothes and fabrics. They work from studios in Nottingham and Cambridge where they design and hand screen-print lengths of fabric, and then make them up into garments.

Christine and Shirley have been interested in art and design since their schooldays. They both did a one-year foundation course in art and design, followed by a three-year degree course in textile design at Nottingham Polytechnic, Nottingham. Although the degree course taught them to design textiles, it was largely biased towards a career in large commercial studios or industrial printers, rather than one in a small, individual studio. Christine and Shirley were encouraged to produce ideas and designs on paper which were then translated into printed textiles by an experienced college technician. This gave them little direct experience of handling dyes and equipment, processing screens, costing and printing fabrics. Determined to acquire the knowledge required to set up their own studio, Christine and Shirley worked closely with the technician, read handbooks on equipment, costing products, contracts and copyrighting, and visited other small studios.

On leaving college, Christine and Shirley set up a small studio and retail shop in Nottingham. There they designed, printed, made and sold unusual and exclusive ranges of designer garments and fabrics directly to the public.

More recently, the pair have moved into the wholesale business, selling smaller ranges of commercial and designer clothing to shops throughout the Midlands and East Anglia. In addition, they work to commission, producing one-off garments for personal customers, and print fabric lengths for fellow textile designers.

Christine and Shirley's daily routine is varied and demanding. One day they might be designing or printing in their studios; the next, out selling their merchandise to shops or through craft fairs. Whatever they are doing, Christine and Shirley enjoy the freedom and rewards of running their own business, although it takes complete dedication to earn a good living. On reflection, both agree that an initial spell in industry, though good experience, may have made them reluctant to give up a secure and salaried job in order to go it alone.

Christine and Shirley's advice to someone starting out is to do a textile design course at an art school or polytechnic or to gain industrial experience. Whatever the approach, both stress the need to work hard, keep learning and to take constant advice.

Design/Product Manager

Christine is the design and product manager for Coats Viyella International Trading, a new venture within Coats Viyella. The company supplies clothing to major retail outlets, including Marks and Spencer PLC.

On leaving school, Christine worked in her father's factory and gained invaluable commercial experience. She then won a scholarship to study fine art for two years at L'Ecole Nationale Supérieure des Beaux-Arts in Paris.

Disillusioned by the absence of good career prospects for even the most talented artists, Christine returned to England to do a degree course in textile design at Manchester Polytechnic. This introduced a more vocational aspect to her education. On leaving college, Christine joined a small, specialist knitwear manufacturer. There she designed a wide range of knitwear and helped to run the company's production schedules. With such industrial experience, Christine decided to freelance and spent two years working on her own design projects. But the lure of big business tempted her to move back into industry. After many inquiry letters, Christine was invited to join the design department of a leading menswear manufacturer which is now part of the Coats Viyella group. There, she handled the company's business with Marks and Spencer PLC and, two years later, joined Coats Viyella International Trading as a design and product manager.

Christine's work is stimulating and challenging, and she particularly values the mix of commercial and creative design skills that it requires. Christine's role is to identify new market opportunities and develop successful new products; oversee production schedules and product quality; and to keep abreast of fashion trends and competitors. Although rewarding, such a role is very demanding. Christine constantly has to meet tight and inflexible deadlines, and produce commercial but stylish merchandise that is guaranteed to sell well, at a specific price!

Christine believes that a successful career, in whatever field, requires a combination of determination and opportunism:

> It is easy, and tragic, to be deflected from what you really want to do by the well-intentioned opinions of others. The flexibility to take alternative approaches to your goal, and alertness to the opportunities constantly presenting themselves, are vital qualities for success in a rapidly changing industry.

Fashion Journalist

Sarah Mower is associate editor for *Vogue* magazine in London. Working with a team of fashion editors and their assistants, Sarah edits and writes the magazine's monthly fashion articles.

Sarah studied English and art history at Leeds University, intending to become a writer and journalist. She was always interested in fashion and was a runner-up in a *Vogue* talent contest for young writers but, at this stage, did not expect to become a fashion journalist. On leaving university, Sarah joined *Ms London* magazine as a general dogsbody. There she researched and wrote about anything and everything, from a weekly shopping column to a budget fashion page. Gradually Sarah worked her way up and, by liaising closely with the magazine's editor, learnt the basics of good journalism. Sarah's ability to research and write well then led to a series of jobs on leading magazines and newspapers, including the *Guardian*, the *Observer* and, more recently, *Vogue*.

Sarah sees herself as a journalist interested in fashion rather than a specialist fashion journalist. She believes that fashion, like any other subject, requires good intellectual inquiry into all its facets. A good journalist should not treat fashion as something ephemeral, concerned only with style, but as an important subject with political, economic, social, sexual and cultural connotations. In her own work, Sarah tries not to be merely descriptive (for example, 'This is a stunning green coat with fur collar designed by . . .') but explores how and why designers get their new ideas, and how these might change and develop in the future.

Sarah's main role begins when she visits the international fashion shows in London, Milan, New York and Paris. For four weeks, twice a year, she has to look at, analyse and write about over 150 new designer collections for Spring and Autumn. Although this sounds glamorous and exciting, it requires complete concentration and dedication. A misreported detail or fact could lead to problems for both Sarah and the magazine. On her return, Sarah discusses her findings and reports with her fellow editors. Together, they create appropriate fashion stories, themes or looks to feature in the magazine, and liaise with stylists, models and photographers to put them into practice.

Sarah's advice to someone starting out in fashion journalism is to learn to write clearly and concisely; to learn to type; to look constantly at fashion magazines, films and exhibitions in order to understand what influences fashion design; to write articles about fashion and send them to fashion editors; to be prepared to start at the bottom and work up and, above all, to be determined. Sarah stresses that, at the moment, there is a shortage of good young fashion journalists and, for a person with the above qualities, there are many potential opportunities.

Fashion Assistant/Stylist

Julie Donelly is the fashion assistant to the fashion editor of *Mail and Femail* magazine.

Julie did a four-year sandwich course in fashion communication and promotion at St Martin's School of Art in London. During the first year, Julie studied fashion and textile design, tailoring and garment construction and pattern cutting. Although this introduced her to every aspect of fashion design, and has since been invaluable, Julie was frustrated because she wanted to write. During the second year, however, Julie was able to concentrate on writing and, under the guidance of well-known visiting journalists and editors, covered almost every style and area of fashion journalism.

Julie's third year was spent on work experience, and her first placement was with *Family Circle* magazine. There, Julie learnt the basics of fashion editing and writing. This included how to compile stories, how to order clothes from public relations departments, how to style (i.e. put together) clothes, how to book photographers and models, how to compile stockists' lists and devise captions, and how to meet the readers' style and price requirements. From *Family Circle*, Julie moved to the *Clothes Show* magazine where she met her current editor. Julie now had to consider a young and highly fashionable reader with no limited budgets.

Julie's final placement was in the public relations department of Dickins and Jones, the London department store. There, Julie liaised with fashion editors and stylists who borrowed clothes from the store to feature in their articles. Julie not only built up a large contact list, but learnt what a stylist looks for when devising a fashion story. At this stage, Julie should have returned to college for a final year, but was invited back to the *Clothes Show* magazine and then to *Mail and Femail* magazine where she has since remained.

Julie's role is to organize everything for the weekly fashion articles in the magazine. Throughout the fashion season, Julie and her editor visit fashion shows and designer shops to observe fashion trends and compile ideas for fashion stories. These might be based on a theme, lifestyle, colour, silhouette or particular garment, and must be carefully tailored to the readers' interests. Several weeks before each article is printed, Julie visits all the fashion press offices which keep a range of designers' or companies' latest collections, and selects those which fit her particular story. The clothes are then sent to her office, and Julie and her editor finalize exactly how they will style, photograph and write about them. Julie's next task is to book appropriate models, photographers and locations, either in Britain or abroad, and to assemble all the necessary clothes, accessories and props ready for the photographic shoot. Once on location, Julie has to solve any problems which arise, including helping busy hairdressers, calming temperamental models and tactfully directing the photographer so that the photographs look exactly as the editor wants them. On her return, Julie sends back the clothes to the correct press offices, writes the copy and captions for the article, and begins work on the next story.

Julie loves her job because it combines everything in which she is most interested: fashion design, magazines and writing. However, the job requires energy, commitment and an ability to take the blame if things go wrong! Julie's advice to someone starting out as a fashion assistant is to get a strong college background in every aspect of fashion design, to be visually aware and interested in everything to do with art and design; to approach as many fashion editors as possible; and to be quietly determined.

8 Freelancing

Fashion Photographer

Sean Knox is a successful young fashion photographer based in London. His many clients include *Elle* and *Cosmopolitan* magazines.

Sean left school after A levels to study public relations at college. After a year he found that the course was not to his liking and began to consider possible career alternatives. Sean had always been interested in both fashion and photography but, as yet, had no experience of combining the two interests. He decided to contact every fashion photographer in London, hoping to visit their studios to observe them and their assistants at work. As a result, Sean was invited to sit-in on several photographic sessions and this prompted him to leave college to become a photographer's assistant. He joined a fashion photographer, specializing in catalogue work, and suddenly found himself making the tea, cleaning the studio, answering the telephone, cleaning and loading cameras, setting up lighting, meeting clients and models, and bearing the brunt of everything that went wrong!

After a year of this, Sean decided to move into editorial fashion photography and joined first Neil Kirk and then Martin Brading, two top London photographers. While working for Brading, Sean picked up as many technical tips as possible, and persuaded several leading agencies to lend him models to photograph in his spare time. In this way, Sean built up a small but high quality portfolio, and set up on his own at home, hiring outside studios only for photographic shoots. Gradually, Sean's client list increased from just a few teenage and women's magazines to include the full range of top fashion magazines. His plans are now to gain more experience, work abroad and to attract international and advertising clients.

Sean enjoys the flexibility of working for himself, travelling abroad, meeting all kinds of people and being well paid for what he does. He does not enjoy long and often unsocial hours. Sean's advice to someone starting out is to become a photographer's assistant and learn as much as possible from the photographer; to take pictures constantly and build up a good portfolio, and to be friendly but determined.

Fashion Illustrator

Nicky Dupays is a self-employed, freelance illustrator. She specializes in fashion and beauty illustration. Her clients include British Home Stores, Burberrys, *Cosmopolitan*, Design Intelligence, *Elle*, the *Guardian*, Gordon Fraser cards, *Mail on Sunday*, Mosquito Fashion, *New Woman*, Octopus Books, *She*, *Sunday Express* magazine, Tesco Stores, Tierack Stores, and many other magazines and companies.

While at school, Nicky did life-drawing at evening classes and this inspired her to go to art college. She did a one-year foundation course followed by a three-year degree course in fashion and textile design at Gloucestershire College of Art. The degree course aimed to produce fashion designers and pattern cutters, and many students were unaware of the other career opportunities in the fashion industry, including fashion illustration. However, Nicky's training in fashion design has since proved invaluable. It has helped her to understand every aspect of the garments which she now has to illustrate.

Nicky works from a studio at home in London. She sets her own timetable, has relative creative freedom and flexibility, is paid well for what she enjoys doing, and meets all kinds of people. Every day is different, and even the most boring job can be turned into a challenge. However, in order to meet tight deadlines and make a good living, Nicky has to work extremely hard. She often works late into the evening and over weekends, and finds that this can disrupt her home and social life. Over the years, Nicky has learnt to cope with criticism of her work, especially when a critical client is paying the bill!

The only part of her work which Nicky dislikes is the administration, including accounts, sending off work to new clients and exhibitions, and following up unpaid bills.

Despite the rather unworldly image of the artist, Nicky stresses that a professional designer or illustrator must be organized and businesslike. Her plans are to improve and diversify her work, and to work with art directors in Europe and America.

Nicky's advice to someone starting out is to design and print a distinctive business card, and to prepare a well-presented portfolio containing a few good and varied pieces of work. These might include a range of different illustrative styles in colour and black and white, and a set of personal projects to show how the styles might be used. Once the portfolio is ready, look at illustrations in all the fashion magazines and contact the most appropriate art directors. Even though magazine work is poorly paid, it is the best way of getting new illustrations widely seen. Be polite, persistent, punctual and try never to miss a deadline.

Jewellery Designer

Louise is a young self-employed jeweller who designs and makes non-precious jewellery. Her designs are modern and appeal to design shops and galleries as well as to fashion retail outlets. She has a workshop in London where the jewellery is designed by Louise and assembled by assistants.

Louise went to an academic school at which art and design were viewed as irrelevant, recreational subjects. Louise gave up art for physics but continued to make things at home. On leaving school, Louise took a year out of education and worked in Switzerland. She was so impressed by the high standard of design there that she returned to England to study at art college and became a self-employed designer. Louise did a one-year foundation course during which she was given a good grounding in drawing, sculpture, photography, film-making, jewellery, ceramics, print-making, fashion and textiles. Louise enjoyed working meticulously and on a small scale, and decided to study silversmithing and jewellery at Sheffield City Polytechnic. For the first year, Louise found the course limiting and restrictive, especially after such an exciting foundation course. She studied metal techniques, gemology and art history. During the second and third years, however, the course improved and Louise was able to experiment and pursue her own design projects. All too soon it was degree time and the end of the course.

Louise was out in the real world with no job, little money, no help and no tools or machinery which she had taken for granted at college. With little business knowledge, Louise set up in 1979 with £400 which bought a work-bench and a few hand-tools. Her first collection was made entirely by hand from cheap, colourful materials bought from local stationery shops, including plastic, card, gift-wrapping ribbons and wood. Louise found addresses of suitable London shops by looking at stockists' lists in fashion magazines, and took her collection to as many shops as possible. It sold well. She also showed at trade fairs and attracted many new customers that way.

In 1984, Louise received a huge order from a Japanese department store, and had to change her production methods in order to make larger quantities. This enabled her to expand, employ an assistant and move to London.

For the last few years, Louise has worked entirely in plastics – their colour and lightness are ideal for jewellery. Most of the machining is done in factories outside the workshop, but each piece is still finished and assembled by hand. Louise's jewellery now sells in America, Japan, Switzerland and Germany. She has no ambitions to expand her business unless a design manager joins her to take over the production and organization, leaving Louise free to design and experiment.

Louise's advice to someone starting out is to make the most of a college training, particularly a foundation course because it is the only opportunity to learn about all aspects of art and design; and to choose the most appropriate college and course by visiting it and talking to the students beforehand.

On leaving college, Louise suggests:

> You should be aware of fashion trends and what sort of jewellery is sold where. Any work that you show should be well made, finished and presented. You will have more confidence if you are proud of the work you are showing. You should take any opportunity to show your work in exhibitions or to prospective clients even if it seems that bit too much effort to get it there on time. You will have to work hard for long hours and little money at first. You may have to spend a lot of time working late on your own and you will need determination to succeed as there is so much competition. You have to keep coming up with new ideas, producing something different yet in keeping with fashion trends

to attract the buyers and publicity in the fashion press. A successful idea will soon be copied and made more cheaply so you must always be one step ahead.

But, she also warns:

> There are huge responsibilities especially to keep the money coming in to pay the bills, and there will be no steady wage for you until the business is established. The temptation to take the nine-to-five job with a wage packet at the end of the week is always there.
>
> However, if you value your independence you will have it, you are your own boss and you can direct your business whichever way you like. If you want to travel you can direct collections at foreign markets. Many opportunities arrive out of the blue as people get to know you and your work and, at the end of the day, it is really satisfying to know that everything has been instigated by you alone.

Costume Maker

Anna French is a freelance costume maker. Anna did a one-year foundation course at Nottingham Polytechnic, followed by a two-year diploma course in theatre wardrobe at Wimbledon College of Art, London. The diploma course introduced Anna to all aspects of costume making, including drawing, pattern cutting, garment construction, wig making and millinery. She was tutored by leading costume designers and makers.

On leaving college, Anna became an assistant to a freelance costume maker. She worked closely with a costume designer to make stunning but wearable opera and ballet costumes for several professional productions. After eighteen months, Anna took a year off and spent it in Italy, drawing and finding new inspiration for her costume designs. She then returned to England and moved into freelance fashion design. Using her technical knowledge and Italian inspiration, Anna designed and made her own collections of clothes and took them to several designer shops to sell. Although this was creatively exciting, it was not financially rewarding, and a year ago Anna decided to go back to theatrical work. She telephoned every theatrical contact she could find and has since had a steady stream of work. This has included making costumes for a leading French ballet company, producing intricate embroidered cloaks for the Moscow State Ballet; making punk rat costumes for a pantomime at Nottingham Playhouse, and many other unusual projects.

Anna's role is to make theatrical costumes according to the exact requirements of the costume designer, the choreographer, if there is one, and the actor or actress. She discusses the designer's drawings with him or her, is given all the necessary measurements and fabrics, and makes up the costume to a 'first fitting' standard. The actor or actress tries on the costume and Anna and the designer make any required changes to it. Anna then completes the costume ready for a dress parade or dress rehearsal. This enables her to make any small last-minute changes, and to see the costume being worn on the stage and under theatrical lighting. This can sometimes be disappointing if, for example, the lighting changes the colour of a costume. Anna's job requires sensitivity and an ability to interpret and translate a designer's drawing into a real costume. For this reason, a good costume maker is highly valued by a costume designer, and Anna is well paid for what she does. She works hard and never quite knows what she might have to do next!

Anna's advice to someone starting out in costume making is to do a college course in costume design, theatre design or theatre ward-robe and then to gain as much theatrical experience as possible.

Milliner

Kirsten Woodward is a leading hat designer with her own workshop and retail shop in London.

Kirsten did a four-year course in fashion design at the London College of Fashion. The course included fashion design, pattern cutting, garment construction, millinery, life-drawing, Italian, busi-ness studies, sociology and communications. Although Kirsten found the practical tuition invaluable, the business and theoretical studies concerned only large companies and were irrelevant to Kirsten's interest in setting up a small, independent business. Infor-mation about book-keeping, tax and self-promotion would have been more useful. On leaving college, Kirsten and four fellow stu-dents rented a stall at Hyper Hyper, the avant-garde fashion emporium in Kensington High Street, London. There they sold their individual collections including hats, accessories, knitwear and separates. Quite unexpectedly, Kirsten was discovered at Hyper Hyper by Karl Lagerfeld, the top Paris-based fashion designer. He invited her to design a range of hats for his new collection, due to be launched in a few weeks! Kirsten worked harder than she ever had before. The hats were a great success and Kirsten has worked for Lagerfeld ever since, gaining widespread recognition and credibility in the fashion world.

Kirsten's advice to someone starting out is to put together a small collection of work; to target it at the relevant buyers, shops and magazines; to be well organized and well presented; and to be quietly and politely persistent. Kirsten's motto is always: nothing ventured, nothing gained.

Shoe Designer/Maker

Emma Hope is a leading shoe designer and maker based in London.

Emma was always interested in fashion design. At school she received a good general background in art and design, and opted for a creative rather than an academic career. At this time, exciting designer shoes were beginning to be imported from Italy and as no one in Britain was designing or making such shoes, Emma saw this as a promising career opportunity.

On leaving school, Emma attended Cordwainers College in Hackney, London, the only college to offer a comprehensive technical course in shoe design and manufacture. There, Emma learnt about the anatomy of feet; technical drawing; pattern making; leather sourcing, cutting and machining – in short, everything required to turn a sketch into a practical and comfortable 'working' shoe. Although such technical input was excellent, the course was less good in the creative aspects of shoe design, including colour, shape, style and decoration; and in its career and business advice. It was assumed that all the students would go into large-scale manufacturing industries in Britain or Italy, and there was little help for students, like Emma, planning to set up small businesses to produce handmade designer shoes. This was viewed as unworldly and idealistic.

Determined, Emma left Cordwainers to set up her own business in Islington, London. She found an experienced accountant to assist with tax and book-keeping and gradually built up her enterprise to employ three adaptable and reliable staff. Emma now runs a workshop in which she designs and makes shoes; a wholesale business which distributes her shoes to buyers and shops throughout Britain, America, Australia, Japan and the Middle East; and an exclusive retail shop which sells Emma's shoes direct to the customer.

At the beginning of each season, Emma designs several collections of men's and women's shoes, including special wedding shoes. The women's shoes are handmade for her by a team of shoe-makers in a small factory in London, and the men's shoes are made up in Northampton, the centre of British shoe manufacture. Alongside shoes for her own business, Emma also designs and has made special footwear collections to accompany the work of well-known fashion designers, including Betty Jackson and John Flett.

Three months before the new Autumn fashion season, Emma meets the designers to discuss ideas, colours, fabrics and silhouettes. This can sometimes prove difficult. At this stage, the designers may still be unsure of what they will eventually produce in their next collections. Emma must pull together the initial ideas and, in a few weeks, produce first a range of complementary sample shoes for the designers' approval, and finally, a range of perfected 'cat-walk' shoes. These are worn in the Autumn fashion shows and enable buyers to place orders with Emma or the designers.

Emma's job has many advantages and disadvantages. She enjoys being self-employed and her own boss, but finds the constant pressure of deadlines, production schedules, administration, meeting orders, overseeing her new shop and so on, takes her further away from the drawing board than she would like, and leaves little time for a home and social life. She plans to open more shops, develop her wholesale business and work with a wider range of fashion designers.

Her advice to someone starting out is to get as much business advice as possible; to establish a good work schedule and always to meet deadlines; and to be a good judge of character.

Textile Designer

Tamar Craggs is a young, self-employed textile designer who has run her own business, 'The Designerie', from home since 1986.

After O levels at school, Tamar did a two-year BTEC National Diploma in general art and design, followed by a three-year degree course in printed textiles at Duncan of Jordanstone College of Art in Dundee, Scotland. There, she studied all aspects of printed textile design, including the experimental and creative aspects, and the more technical aspects of handling dyes, understanding printing processes, and so on. While at college, Tamar won a travel award and this enabled her to try out work placements in several different design studios. As a result, Tamar gained not only valuable work experience, but also a greater insight into the career opportunities available to her. On leaving college, Tamar returned to one of the design studios to work part time and used her spare time to develop her own design work. Gradually her own work took over completely and Tamar set up her own freelance business, 'The Designerie', using the Enterprise Allowance Scheme to do so.

Working one, or even two, years ahead of the fashion season, Tamar produces textile ideas and designs on paper which she sells to a variety of regular clients, including textile manufacturers and printers, retail companies and design studios. They then translate the paper ideas and designs into finished products. These might be, for example, fashion fabrics, furnishing fabrics, wallpaper or T-shirt designs – almost anything with a decorative surface pattern. In addition, Tamar also designs and organizes the printing of her own exclusive range of greetings cards and teaches part time at a local art college. Although Tamar's work is incredibly varied, she finds that working freelance has several advantages and disadvantages.

The disadvantages are the irregular money, long hours, constant administration, and the motivation and self-discipline needed to work from home and alone, and constantly to find new work. The advantages are the flexibility to work how and when she likes, the immense variety of work and the excitement of getting a good project and doing it well.

Tamar's advice to any would-be fashion and textile designer is to gain as much industrial experience as possible, and to be aware of the immense difference between a college training and real industry. She also stresses the importance of finding out about running a small business before embarking on a career as a self-employed designer.

Textile Artist

Kaffe Fassett is an internationally acclaimed textile artist based in London. He is a knitwear designer and maker; needlepoint designer and stitcher; and designer for the decorative arts, including printed textiles, wallpaper, ceramics, tin boxes, greetings cards and stationery. He is also a well-known lecturer and television presenter, and has written several books on knitting and needlepoint.

Kaffe had only six months' formal art school training in fine art, and no training in textile design. Instead, he was very much influenced by his surroundings, and found growing up in an area of California where everyone designed and built their own houses, knitted, sewed, made pots, painted, and so on, to be more stimulating and inspiring. His interest in knitting began when he came to Britain and discovered the wonderful colours in Scottish Shetland yarns. At this stage, no one was producing exciting, multi-coloured knitting so Kaffe took up the challenge. The other areas of design in which he is now involved just followed on as his work developed and he experimented with different media.

Kaffe works around the clock and at most weekends, but finds this to be the most creatively satisfying way of living. He constantly creates new designs and has help with the more tedious elements of turning designs into kits, or compiling them into books. Kaffe also enjoys the added satisfaction of having inspired a growing audience of knitters and needlepoint artists. His future plans are to do more television programmes, write more books, give more lectures, and, above all, produce even more ambitious and 'over the top' designs!

His advice to someone starting out is:

> When in doubt, overdo it. Most design is a little timid – add more richness and extreme style to your work – you can always pare down or simplify later. Get your wildest, most personal thoughts and feelings out into the world.

Weaver/Knitwear Designer

Susie Freeman is a freelance weaver and knitwear designer and maker whose work bridges the gap between art or craft and fashion. Her clothes are often displayed in craft galleries, but they are also fun to wear. Susie works from her own studio in London.

Susie did a one-year foundation course followed by a degree in woven textiles at Manchester Polytechnic. She then went on to the Royal College of Art where she specialized in woven and knitted textiles. Susie's foundation course gave her a sound basis in observation and drawing, and an ability to stretch ideas in many directions. She regards this as the most imaginative and exciting part of her design education. Susie's degree course was quite technical and gave her a basic training in woven structures, knitting and related craft techniques, including spinning, weaving, vegetable dyeing and macramé. However, it gave her little business advice or industrial experience in terms of work placements, visits to manufacturers or lectures from practising designers.

At the Royal College of Art, Susie was left very much to her own devices and moved towards knitwear design. There, a personal project led to the development of sequinned fabrics and semi-transparent knitted pocket structures. On leaving college, Susie used a Crafts Council Grant to set up her own workshop. She developed the college project and, using an industrial knitting machine, used fine nylon to knit a fabric of 'pockets'. Into each pocket, Susie put a different tiny object – fragment of wool, foil, ribbon or fabric; a piece of shiny plastic, a sequin or a shell. Depending on what was in the pockets and the basic colour of the fabric, Susie created unlimited variations of exotic, shimmering cloths which she then fashioned into a range of exclusive garments and accessories.

Susie's work has been widely exhibited. Her skills as a freelance designer have enabled her to design exclusive collections for the American and Japanese fashion markets; and to design costumes for film and television. She also produces a range of smaller, more affordable items such as neck cowls and bow ties.

Susie enjoys the creative freedom and flexibility of her work, but stresses that the hours are long and that the income is erratic and relatively small. Her advice to someone starting out in the same area is to do a foundation course followed by a degree in fashion and textile design; to visit relevant colleges and courses to see which are suitable; to find out about setting-up grants, or share a workshop with friends; to work very hard, and to keep an ideas book for the more uninspired days!

Fashion Designer

Wendy Dagworthy is a leading fashion designer, and head of the three-year BA(Hons) fashion course at St Martins School of Art in London.

Wendy did a foundation course at Medway College of Art, followed by a degree course in fashion design at Middlesex Polytechnic. The degree course had excellent tutors and, in three years, Wendy learnt how to design, pattern cut and construct clothing – in short, how to turn an idea into a wearable garment. She did not, though, learn very much about business.

On leaving college, Wendy joined the design team at Radley, a major clothing manufacturer who produced ranges for well-known designers, including Ossie Clark. There, she soon learnt about the commercial aspects of the fashion industry. At the same time, Wendy continued to design and make clothes at home and, through a friend, produced a set of stage clothes for Roxy Music who were just starting out. These were so successful that Wendy took some similar clothes to London shops. They sold well and she decided to start her own business. Working from home, Wendy designed and made a co-ordinated collection of women's jackets, shirts, skirts, suits and trousers and, once again, took them to several London shops. As orders increased, Wendy could no longer work alone and from home. With a small bank loan, she took on a pattern cutter, machinist and assistant, and set up her own studio and company, Wendy Dagworthy Ltd. Wendy's aim was to produce unusual, distinctive and comfortable clothes for both men and women: 'You wear them, they don't wear you.'

She developed an unmistakable style using striking or unexpected colour and fabric combinations, surprising details – a hidden pocket or quirky use of buttons, and the highest quality tailoring and finishing. New inspiration was constantly sought through travel, and by looking at and drawing from all kinds of things, from paintings to foreign landscapes. Within two years, Wendy joined the prestigious London Designer Collections, exhibited at international fashion shows, won several awards, and established herself as a leading international designer. She also began to teach and assess at major art colleges.

Throughout, Wendy always managed every aspect of her business, from designing to supervising production schedules and checking accounts. Recently, however, she turned her attention fully to design education, finding the increasing commercial and financial pressures of the fashion industry too much to bear.

Wendy Dagworthy's advice to young designers starting out is to go into industry and learn about every aspect of the fashion world before setting up on their own. Today this requires huge financial backing and a sound commercial knowledge of the international fashion market, two things the young designer rarely has. Wendy also advises young designers to gain work experience in France or Italy where fashion design has a much higher profile, and where there are more potential outlets for their work; to be confident, determined and hard-working, and not to overlook the many other interesting and rewarding careers in the fashion industry, apart from design.

Part 4   Getting into Fashion Design

In Part 4 we look at what you may need to do if you want to get a training in fashion design or management. We also discuss practical issues about getting a job and being aware of the professional organizations and other bodies that can give you help and advice.

9 Have You Got What It Takes?

A job in the world of fashion/textiles design can give opportunities for individuality, self-expression and purpose but also demands high professional standards with commitment and determination. It involves having a real interest in fashion and its production and a willingness to keep up to date with current events, style and technology.

If you choose to go into the mainstream of designing, you need design knowledge, understanding and a high level of practical skills in 'drawing and making'. If you choose to go into other aspects of manufacturing, retailing or marketing you will need design knowledge and understanding and a high level of awareness of how these interact with your particular field.

Most aspects of the job will demand:

- Creative imagination and individual style
- Flexibility and adaptability
- Hard work and perseverance to see the job through often to tight time schedules
- Skills of self-expression and ability to problem-solve
- A business sense, ability to organize, plan and communicate
- A great awareness of colour, form and materials
- Ability to work with other people, to be part of a team, recognizing other points of view and the needs of people

Depending on what you are doing you may need mathematical or scientific knowledge, or languages.

10 Choosing a Way In

As you have already seen, the world of fashion design incorporates many activities varying in scale and size:

- Textile manufacturing
- Garment and accessory manufacture
- Retail and display
- Marketing, advertising and promotion

All offer opportunities for a wide range of interests and skills, allowing the freedom to join at different levels of qualification, to move up the career structure, to change direction and to find different jobs in different parts of the country or world.

There have always been those people who 'made it' without formal training or qualifications but they are generally people of exceptional talent and determination. Today, because of the competitive nature of the fashion world and its deadlines, tight specifications and budget scales and need to 'sell', it is becoming increasingly difficult to get very far without formal qualifications. Traditionally in textiles, fashion and photography there have always been openings for people leaving school to work as an assistant and be trained in the studio, workshop or on the shop floor. For the most part these jobs are to do with supporting the technical or retailing aspects of the design area. It is important for anyone taking this route to consider their future career opportunities and perhaps to take a complementary part-time course offered by the City and Guilds of London Institute.

What it boils down to is that there are only three ways into fashion design:

1 Start on the shop floor
2 Start on the shop floor and get a training at the same time
3 Get a training before looking for your first job

For those who want a training, what course to choose will depend very much on what academic qualifications you have on leaving school, what work experience you might have had and whether you wish to specialize at once or to follow a general course and then specialize. People under eighteen years old are unlikely to gain financial support to study outside their local education authority area and therefore should consult their local college of further education to see what courses are available within their local education authority. There are courses that make provision for mature students to study part time, recognizing that they may not have the required academic qualification. The choice of where to go will be determined by age, entry requirements, qualifications wanted, background, interests and skills that you want to develop by further study and training and the opportunities that might be available at the end of the course.

Whether you decide to go straight into a job or get some training first you will be faced with making an application and going to an interview. There are specific ways of writing a letter of application and it will often be useful to get yourself a business card that is well designed and suggests that you are a professional person. If it is fashion design rather than management that interests you, most employers and all colleges will want to see evidence of what you can do. The usual way of presenting your skill in this area is by putting together an impressive portfolio. You will also need a well-thought-out curriculum vitae explaining who you are and what you have done.

On the next few pages you will find advice and examples that you may want to follow.

The Interview

- Before going for a course interview, find out from people in the field what is involved, or even do a period of apprenticeship, which will help to develop an understanding of the field and more realistic career aims.

- Before going for a job interview, research the company, the type of work it is involved in, and look at their manufacturing line.

- Dress in a businesslike manner, but one that reflects your personality.

- Know the exact time and place of the interview and the interviewer's name and title.

- Prepare questions; interviews are a two-way process.

- Be prepared to answer questions about your abilities and aims.

- Keep to the point and do not over-answer.

- Thank the interviewer for his/her time.

- If a position is offered to you on the spot accept it at once if that is what you want or, if necessary, ask for a specific time to think it over. And call the interviewer with a response whatever the choice.

The Portfolio

A well-presented portfolio is as important to those applying to a design course as it is to those applying for a job in a design-related area.

- It should be a selection of your best work, highlighting your particular design skills. It is a good idea to include concept sketches and roughs as well as finished work.

- It should be well mounted and labelled.

- It is best to use A2 or A3 size portfolios: these are easier to handle than A1 size.

- It may include slides of three-dimensional work or large pieces; actual garments and samples. Have drawings reduced by photocopying if necessary.

- College applicants should review their selection with their teacher, evaluating strengths and weaknesses and what else might need to be done.

- Job applicants should make sure that the selection represents the kind of work the employer is looking for but also the variety to emphasize their particular talents and skills.

- You must feel confident with your work and be able to talk about it freely.

- Be very careful about forwarding or leaving your portfolio. Never include your only copy. If you do, take slides and/or photocopies of it.

The Curriculum Vitae

A c.v. is a brief resumé of your education, and experience relevant to the college or job application.

- Use plain, good quality paper.

- Have it typed or word processed, make sure there are no spelling mistakes.

- Think about the layout and set the information out clearly.

- Begin with name, address, telephone number, date of birth.

- Put details of education, qualifications and awards.

- List work experience by date and employer. Put the most recent job first with brief description.

- State languages spoken.

- Personal interests.

- Names and addresses of referees.

- Include a covering letter in your own handwriting – unless it is illegible.

Examples of a covering letter and c.v. follow on pp. 118–20:

21 High Street
Oakham
Leicestershire
LE15 7SU

Telephone 0572 724361

Mr Ronald Jordan
Knitwear International PLC
Swallow Street
London
WC1 3NX

24 April 1989

Dear Mr Jordan

I saw your advertisement for a design assistant in *Design Week*. I have just completed my BA(Hons) Course in Fashion Design and Marketing at Newcastle. I am particularly interested in the post because it offers an opportunity to specialize in knitwear which was the focus of my final year major project. Your innovative range is well known to me and I would like to be associated with it.

I enclose a copy of my curriculum vitae and look forward to hearing from you.

Yours sincerely,

Diana Eagle

CURRICULUM VITAE

NAME	Diana Eagle
ADDRESS	21 High Street Oakham Leicestershire LE15 7SU
TELEPHONE	0572 724361
DATE OF BIRTH	10 December 1965
MARITAL STATUS	Single
NATIONALITY	British

EDUCATION

1985–1988	BA(Hons) 2.1 Fashion Design and Marketing Newcastle-upon-Tyne Polytechnic
1984–1985	Foundation course Loughborough College of Art and Design
1980–1984	Oadby Upper School Oadby, Leicester
	GCE A Levels Design English History
	GCE O Levels Mathematics English language English literature Art Biology French

WORK EXPERIENCE

| 1984 | Summer vacation work at Next in Leicester |
| 1986–1987 | Summer vacation work in the studio at Textile Design Ltd, Nottingham |

REFERENCES

Professor Margery Hendricks
Dean of Fashion Design
Newcastle-upon-Tyne Polytechnic
Newcastle
Tyne and Wear
NE1 8ST

John Baxendale
Managing Director
Textile Design Ltd
Trent Bridge Industrial Estate
Nottingham
NG2 4BU

INTERESTS

Cinema
History of fashion
Swimming
Photography

REMEMBER! A c.v. needs to be up to date and sometimes adapted to the particular job you are applying for. It presents a snapshot of you and what you have done. Keep a photocopy of it, together with your letter of application.

11 Choosing a Course

The British education system provides a great variety of courses. This should make it possible to select a course which is well tailored to each person's needs. Unfortunately it can also be confusing. It is not always easy to find out what is on offer or whether it is at an appropriate level. Added to that, the pattern of courses in Scotland and Northern Ireland is distinctly different from that in England and Wales.

The variety of courses can be discussed in three main ways:

- The type of qualification offered
- The subject area
- The route, duration and place of study

Qualifications

The most fundamental distinction is between degree and non-degree courses. In general terms, degree courses will aim to give a broad, academic view of the subject matter while non-degree courses will be more directly related to specific technological or business requirements. However, there are sandwich courses at degree level that include a substantial experience of industry, and non-degree courses that provide good general training.

Many institutions offer a package of courses covering a variety of levels and qualifications. The majority of degree courses in fashion and textiles design are to be found in the art and design faculties of polytechnics or in colleges of art and design but there are also interesting courses available in institutes of higher education where it is often possible to study a number of subjects in combination. Business, management and technology can be studied at degree level at universities, polytechnics or institutes of higher education. Non-degree courses are dispersed throughout the education system, some being located in colleges of further education.

The variety of qualifications can be understood by discussing how the courses are approved and validated. There are six main ways:

Universities

Universities are independent institutions with their own Charters. They set their own standards and patterns of degrees at all levels including first degree, postgraduate and Ph.D. They can also validate degrees taken in other colleges, particularly institutes of higher education.

The Council for National Academic Awards

The CNAA is the body responsible for validating degree courses outside the university sector. Its awards cover the whole range of degree-level work and, in relation to fashion, include design, business, management and technology courses. The CNAA deals with polytechnics, colleges of art and design and institutes of higher education throughout Great Britain.

The Business and Technician Education Council

BTEC covers England, Wales and Northern Ireland and is responsible for non-degree courses. The Council's role is to 'advance the quality and availability of work-related education' for those in, or preparing for, employment. There are courses at General, National, Higher National and Post-experience levels. BTEC deals with polytechnics, colleges of art and design, institutes of higher education and further education colleges.

The Scottish Vocational Education Council

In Scotland, SCOTVEC plays a similar role to BTEC, validating General, Specialist, Multi-disciplinary and Higher National Certificates and Diplomas. These courses are found in colleges of further education.

Professional Bodies and Institutions

Many design courses will give you Diploma membership of the Chartered Society of Designers and this can be converted to full membership if you remain in practice. The Clothing and Footwear Institute sponsors a number of courses which offer a Management Diploma and which give you the status of an Associate of the Institute.

Local Education Authorities and Colleges

LEAs and individual colleges can validate their own courses at sub-degree level, often in relation to particular local needs or industries. All the one-year foundation courses in art and design that act as a bridge between school and degree courses are validated in this way.

The City and Guilds of London Institute

City and Guilds validates a great variety of specialist, technological and craft courses many of which can be taken part time or in direct relation to employment.

Further information is readily available from all these organizations in the form of leaflets, annual reports and lists of courses. For universities, the Universities Central Council on Admissions (UCCA) issues a list of all undergraduate courses in Great Britain.

Addresses

The Universities Central Council on Admissions (UCCA)
PO Box 28
Cheltenham
Gloucestershire GL50 1HY

Publications
How to Apply for Admission to a University (annual publication)
Annual Report
Mature Students and Universities (free)

Standing Conference on University Entrance
29 Tavistock Square
London WC1H 9EZ

Publications
Thinking about University (free)
Qualifying for University Entrance (free)

Scottish Universities Council on Entrance
12 The Links
St Andrews
Fife KY16 9JB

Publication
Scottish Universities Entrance Guide (annual publication)

The Council for National Academic Awards
344–345 Gray's Inn Road
London WC1X 8BP

Publications (from the Publications Officer)
Directory of First Degree and Diploma of Higher Education Courses (free)
Guide for Applicants (annual publication)
Directory of Postgraduate and Post-experience Courses (free)
Annual Report

Committee of Directors of Polytechnics
Kirkman House
12–14 Whitfield Street
London W1P 6AX

Publication
Polytechnics Courses Handbook (published annually)

Business and Technician Education Council
Central House
Upper Woburn Street
London WC1H 0HH

Publication
Higher National Diploma Courses in Design and Associated Studies

Scottish Vocational Education Council
Hanover House
24 Douglas Street
Glasgow G2 7NQ

Publications
Advanced Courses: Technology
Working Together (joint courses, SCOTVEC and City and Guilds)
The Way to a Brighter Future: SCOTVEC's National Certificate (free)

City and Guilds of London Institute
76 Portland Place
London W1N 4AA

Publications
Qualify for Careers in Clothing, Footwear and Leather Goods (free:
quote FR–00–310)
A Brief Guide to City and Guilds (quote FR–00–3002)
List of Publications (quote FR–00–3003)

The Design Council publishes an excellent annual guide to design
courses in Britain at all levels and in every field:
The Design Council
28 Haymarket
London SW1Y 4SU

Publication
Design Courses in Britain (published annually)

Subject Area

The subject area you choose will not only affect your eventual career,
it will also determine the character of the educational experience
you have. Here the most obvious distinction is between design
courses and courses in business or technology.

In all fashion and textile design courses, at whatever level, the major element is studio work. You learn to design by actually designing, often structuring your learning round a series of highly realistic briefs. You will normally have access to the equipment needed to realize your designs and some colleges and polytechnics are very well equipped with production machinery. The final stage of a design course will nearly always entail arranging an exhibition of your best work and, in fashion design, taking part in a full-scale fashion show. This is the acid test. Passing the course will be dependent on the quality of the products you create and the intelligence and originality with which you meet the requirements. The same applies to photography, illustration and graphic design – you learn by doing.

Most full-time design courses, in whatever subject area, will also demand that you study the history of art and design, develop general drawing and communication skills, come to grips with the relevant technology, learn something about business practice and write clearly.

Many of the better-known design courses are hard to get on to with many more applicants than places. They are also highly competitive within themselves, particularly as the time for the final exhibition or fashion show approaches. Students know that employers use the big degree shows to look for talent and they are determined to make as big an impression as they can.

It is important to realize that there is great variety within the provision of design courses. Some will be best suited to educate designer-makers who want to set up a small business for themselves and build a modest livelihood around being their own boss, others will prepare the energetic, go-getting high-flyer for that first important plunge into the hectic world of international fashion design. Others again will give exactly the kind of sound aesthetic and business background needed to work on designs for the high street chains. Choose carefully and be prepared to shop around before finally selecting the course that suits your plans for the future.

If you choose to study business or management as your way into the fashion industry, you will find a greater amount of theory in your course, although business courses more and more use realistic role-play and simulation as a way of relating theory to practice. Many involve periods of attachment to industry and use management projects as one of the means of learning. If your emphasis is on technology and production, the theory you learn will be directly related to the qualities of yarns and dyes, the machinery used in the industry, computer-aided pattern grading and cutting and the interaction between the various stages of the production process.

There are no universities, colleges or polytechnics that offer the complete range of possible courses in relation to fashion design and management. The one that comes nearest to achieving this is the London College of Fashion. It is one of three monotechnical colleges established in London over the years: the others deal with the furniture and printing industries. It is a part of the London Institute and offers students an environment for study that is entirely devoted to fashion. This has drawbacks as well as advantages. Fashion designers and managers need to be aware of general cultural and business developments as a background to their particular concerns and this may be easier to achieve in a multi-faceted art and design college. On the other hand, having students from every area of fashion is unique to this particular college.

A criticism that can be levelled at universities and polytechnics is that although they have a great variety of courses, students do not always mix easily and inter-departmental contacts are few. The sad truth is that there is often a particularly deep divide between technologists and designers. Institutions are becoming more aware of the dangers of isolating one area from another and there now exist at least a few interdisciplinary courses.

Route, Duration and Place of Study

There are five main routes through further and higher education and on into the fashion industry. Although it is in theory possible to cross over from one to another, in practice this rarely happens and the routes turn out to be surprisingly self-contained. What determines each route is a combination of the end-qualification and the place of study. Each route has a particular time-scale.

Universities

A conventional route into industry has always been to take a general course at university, get a good first degree and then apply for a junior management job or management training. This remains a possible course of action but it is becoming very much more common to study business or management at university, rather than a general course. Universities also offer a small number of excellent specialist first degree courses in textiles, technology and production, occasionally related to management and design. Today, universities often welcome mature students and offer opportunities for study in mid-career. Very few universities run design courses, the main exception being the University of Ulster in Belfast.

It is usual to enter an undergraduate course at university direct from school at eighteen. Most first degree courses leading to the award of the BA (Hons) or B.Sc. (Hons) will last for three or four years. You can go straight from university into industry at this point but a few students interested in research may want to stay on to take a higher degree. Alternatively, a higher degree can be taken later in life.

The London Business School offers an excellent range of specialist courses for managers and, in particular, a one-year postgraduate course in design management that is unique in Britain.

Entrance to university is arranged through UCCA (see p. 123 for address).

Polytechnics (Business and Technology Degrees)

Polytechnics offer basically the same range of first and higher degree courses as universities and have developed some particularly good technology courses. Entry age and duration of study are the same as for university degrees. Entrance to these courses is arranged through the Polytechnics Central Admission System (PCAS), PO Box 67, Cheltenham, Gloucestershire GL50 3AP.

Diversified Degrees

The institutes of higher education specialize in what are known as diversified degrees. This allows students, who enter direct from school at eighteen, to combine subject area modules when planning their three-year course of study. For example, fashion and textiles can be linked directly with business studies and social administration. Many of the relevant courses are located in home economics or art and design departments and students can move on to more specialist postgraduate courses through the Polytechnics Central Admission System (PCAS; see p. 128 for address).

Design – Degree Courses

Before taking a fashion and textile, graphic, illustration or photography first degree course in England and Wales and Northern Ireland, it is usual to do a one-year foundation course. This applies whether you are going to study in a polytechnic faculty of art and design or at a college of art and design. A small number of students (less then ten per cent) go straight from school at eighteen without taking a foundation course. The foundation course acts as a bridge between school and college, enables you to develop your art and design skills and gives you time to choose and apply for a degree course. It is usual to go to a local foundation course because grants are not available for foundation-level study away from home.

The CNAA also accepts a BTEC National Diploma or Certificate as qualifying the holder to apply for admission to a first degree course, so linking the degree and non-degree routes at this point.

In Scotland, the first degree course will last four years and incorporates a foundation element. Entry is direct from school as for all other degree courses.

A great variety of design courses exist, some incorporating a period of attachment in industry. Courses last for between three and four years. There are opportunities to study for higher degrees at a number of polytechnics and particularly at the Royal College of Art which is a unique university institution devoted exclusively to postgraduate work in art and design.

Entrance to foundation courses is by local application. Entrance to degree courses is arranged through the Art and Design Admissions Registry, Penn House, 9 Broad Street, Hereford HR4 9AP.

Design – Non-degree Courses

General art and design courses can be entered from school at sixteen and provide two years of foundation study for students interested in pursuing a design career. Some, fulfilling the traditional role of foundation courses, can be entered in the second year at eighteen. Following this there exists a great variety of two-year full-time and three-year sandwich courses covering the range from fashion and textile design to textile technology.

For further information about these courses, write to the Business and Technician Education Council; in Scotland write to the Scottish Vocational Education Council (see pp. 124 and 125 for addresses).

In the next chapter we list those design, business and technology courses at degree and HND level that are directly related to the fashion and textile industry. We do not list general business or technology courses, foundation or general art and design courses. Further information on all these can be obtained from the addresses and publications listed above.

Distance Learning

Those interested in design and business courses using distance learning should contact the Open University, the Open College or the Open College of the Arts.

The Open University
Walton Hall
Milton Keynes MK7 6AA

The Open College
101 Wigmore Street
London W1H 9AA

The Open College of the Arts
18 Victoria Park Square
London E2 9PF

In general, courses run by these three open institutions will not
equip you to practise fashion design, but they can provide valuable
background knowledge on design, business and management.

12 Entry Requirements and Lists of Courses

Entry Requirements

It is only possible to give a general picture of entry requirements. There is strong competition for places on all courses and individual institutions may set academic standards that are higher than average. On the other hand, a candidate with really remarkable design ability may be admitted without reaching the minimum examination requirements. For design courses, a good portfolio will be essential.

Mature students, people over the age of twenty-one, may be admitted without the minimum requirements if they can demonstrate clear ability in the field of study they wish to follow.

It will be wise to contact the colleges of your choice and the relevant clearing house for specific details.

Foundation Courses

It is usually necessary to take a foundation course before taking a first degree course in fashion or textile design.

2 year   Minimum age: 16
         Some courses specify GCSE Grade 3 passes or equivalent

1 year   Minimum age: 17
         5 GCSE Grade 3 passes or equivalent, some may specify 1 A level

In Scotland, the Introductory Course forms part of the 4-year first degree course. Entry is at seventeen years and you will need 5 SCE passes, at least 3 of them at grade H or equivalent.

BTEC Courses in Design (Fashion and Textiles)

National Certificate/Diploma   Minimum age: 16

	4 GCSE Grade 3 passes or equivalent including BTEC first certificates and diplomas, CPVE or a foundation course.
Higher National Certificate/Diploma	Minimum age: 18 Students should normally have completed a BTEC National Certificate or Diploma course or an equivalent or suitable A levels

First Degree Courses in Design (Fashion and Textiles)

BA (Hons)	Minimum age: 18 Usually successful completion of a foundation or equivalent course such as BTEC but a small proportion of students admitted direct from school 5 GCSE Grade 3 passes or equivalent or 3 GCSE Grade 3 + 1 A level or equivalent or 2 GCSE Grade 3 + 2 A levels or equivalent

First Degree Courses in Textile Technology and Management

BA (Hons) B.Sc. (Hons)	Minimum age: 18 2 A levels or equivalent

College Diplomas and Certificates

Apply to each institution for their particular entry requirements

Clothing Management Diplomas

ACFI (Associate of the Clothing and Footwear Institute)	Minimum age: 18 5 GCE subjects including Maths and English + 1 A level

Lists of Courses

This list of courses cannot be exhaustive. There is much innovation in professional training and new courses are always being introduced. The aim in compiling the lists has been to be as up to date as possible but it is still wise to shop around before deciding on a course and it is particularly helpful if you know somebody who has been on the course that interests you and can therefore give an insider's view.

College Certificates

1 year full time

Basingstoke Technical College	Creative clothing
Bristol Old Vic Theatre School	Theatre wardrobe
London College of Fashion	Clothing production Garment making

2 years full time

Cordwainers Technical College, London	Design (footwear)
Eastbourne College of Arts & Technology	Textiles
London College of Fashion	Tailoring

College Diplomas

2 years full time

Burnley College	Fashion
Clarendon College of Further Education, Nottingham	Design (fashion)

Jacob Kramer College, Leeds.	Clothing
Rochdale College of Art	Textiles, fashion & clothing (also part time)
Wimbledon School of Art	Theatre wardrobe

3 years full time

| London College of Fashion | Tailoring |

2 years or 3 years full time, part time or home study

Duncan of Jordanstone College of Art, Dundee	Printed textiles
Tameside College of Technology, Greater Manchester	Design (fashion)
West Nottingham College of Further Education	Design (fashion)

4 years part time

| Gwent College of Higher Education, Newport | Textile & fashion design |

Coldip 4 years sandwich

| London College of Fashion | Clothing management |

BTEC National Certificate

2 years full time

| Belfast College of Technology | Clothing |
| Bournville College of Art, Birmingham | Design (fashion) |

3 years part time

Wigan College of Technology   Design (fashion)

BTEC National Diploma

2 years full time

Barnet College of Further   Design (fashion)
Education, London

Barnfield College, Luton   Design (fashion)

Barnsley College of Art &   Design (surface pattern)
Design

Belfast College of Technology   Clothing

Berkshire College of Art &   Design (fashion)
Design, Maidenhead

Boston College of Further   Design (fashion)
Education

Bournemouth & Poole College   Design (fashion)
of Art & Technology

Bradford & Ilkley Community   Design (fashion)
College

Canterbury College of Art   Design (fashion/textiles)

Cauldon College, Stoke-on-   Design (fashion)
Trent

Central Manchester College,   Clothing
East Manchester Centre

Chesterfield College of   Design (fashion)
Technology & Arts

Cleveland College of Art &   Design (fashion)
Design

Colchester Institute, N. Essex   Clothing

Cordwainers Technical College,   Design (footwear)
London

Coventry Technical College   Design (fashion)

Croydon College   Design (fashion)

Dacorum College, Hemel   Clothing
Hempstead

Derbyshire College of Higher Education	Design (fashion)
Dewsbury College, Batley	Design (surface pattern)
Doncaster Metropolitan Institute of Higher Education	Design (fashion)
East Warwickshire College of Further Education	Design (fashion)
Epsom School of Art & Design	Design (fashion)
Erith College of Technology	Clothing
Gloucestershire College of Art & Technology	Design (fashion)
Granville College, Sheffield	Design (fashion)
Great Yarmouth College of Art & Design	Design (fashion)
Gwent College of Higher Education, Newport	Design (fashion)
Handsworth Technical College, Birmingham	Clothing
Harrogate College of Arts & Technology	Design (textiles)
Hastings College of Arts & Technology	Design (fashion)
Hereford College of Art & Design	Design (fashion)
Hinckley College of Further Education	Clothing
Hounslow Borough College	Design (fashion)
Isle College, Wisbech	Design (fashion)
Jacob Kramer College, Leeds	Clothing
Lincolnshire College of Art & Design	Design (fashion)
Llandrillo Technical College	Fashion/textiles
London College of Fashion	Clothing technology Design (fashion) Design (embroidery)
Loughborough College of Art & Design	Design (fashion)

Medway College of Art & Design, Rochester	Design (fashion, clothing, theatrical costume)
Montgomery College of Further Education	Clothing
Nene College, Northampton	Design (fashion)
Newcastle upon Tyne College of Arts & Technology	Design (fashion)
North Warwickshire College of Technology & Art, Nuneaton	Design (fashion)
Northbrook College Design & Technology, Worthing	Design (fashion)
Oxford College of Further Education	Clothing
Plymouth College of Art & Design	Design (fashion)
Redbridge Technical College	Design (fashion)
Rotherham College of Arts & Technology	Design (fashion/textiles)
Salford College of Technology	Design (fashion)
Salisbury College of Art	Design (fashion/textiles)
Scarborough Technical College	Fashion
Somerset College of Art and Technology, Taunton	Design (fashion)
South Fields College of Further Education, Leicester	Design (fashion)
Southampton Institute of Higher Education	Design (fashion)
Southend College of Technology	Design (fashion)
Southgate Technical College	Clothing
Southport College of Art & Technology	Design (fashion/textiles)
Stafford College of Further Education	Fashion
Stoke-on-Trent College of Further Education	Design (fashion)

Tameside College of Technology, Greater Manchester	Design (fashion)
West Nottinghamshire College of Further Education, Mansfield	Design (fashion)
Wigan College of Technology	Design (fashion)
York College of Arts & Technology	Design (fashion)

3 years full time

| Central Manchester College, East Manchester Centre | Clothing |

BTEC Higher National Certificate

2 years full time

Belfast College of Technology	Clothing
City College, Liverpool	Clothing
Stafford College of Further Education	Fashion
York College of Arts & Technology	Design (fashion)

2 years part time

| Nottingham Polytechnic | Textile technology |

BTEC Higher National Diploma

2 years full time

Amersham College of Further Education	Textiles
Berkshire College of Art & Design, Maidenhead	Design (fashion)
Bolton Institute of Higher Education	Textiles
Chelsea School of Art	Textiles (design)
Cleveland College of Art & Design, Middlesbrough	Design (fashion/textiles)
Croydon College	Design (fashion)

Derbyshire College of Higher Education	Design (textiles)
Dewsbury College, Batley	Design (fashion/surface pattern)
Epsom School of Art & Design	Design (fashion)
Huddersfield Polytechnic	Design (textiles)
Jacob Kramer College, Leeds	Clothing
Kilburn Polytechnic	Fashion (textiles)
London College of Fashion	Design (fashion)
	Clothing technology
	Design (theatre studies)
Manchester Polytechnic	Clothing
Medway College of Art & Design, Rochester	Clothing technology
	Clothing manufacture
	Fashion (design)
Northbrook College, Design & Technology, Worthing	Design (textiles)
Nottingham Polytechnic	Textiles technology
	also part-time
Somerset College of Arts & Technology	Design (textiles)
South Glamorgan Institute of Higher Education, Cardiff	Design
Southampton Institute of Higher Education	Design (fashion)
Stafford College of Further Education	Design (fashion & footwear)
	also part-time
Stockport College of Technology	Design

3 years full time

Newcastle upon Tyne Polytechnic	Business & fashion

SCOTVEC National Certificate

1 year part time

Cardonald College, Glasgow	Clothing
Telford College of Further Education, Edinburgh	Fashion & fabric crafts

2 years full time

Cardonald College, Glasgow — Fashion design with technology & business skills

SCOTVEC Higher National Diploma

1 year full time

Cardonald College, Glasgow — Clothing

Clothing Management Diplomas
4-year Sandwich Course

Barmulloch College of Further
Education, Glasgow
Belfast College of Technology
London College of Fashion
Manchester Polytechnic
Teeside Polytechnic

First Degree Courses

BA (Hons) 3 years full time

Bretton Hall College, School of Art & Design, Wakefield	
Bristol Polytechnic	Textiles/fashion
Camberwell School of Art & Crafts, London	Textiles
Central School of Art & Design, London	Textiles design
City of Birmingham Polytechnic	Textiles/fashion
Duncan of Jordanstone College of Art, Dundee*	Fashion design
Edinburgh College of Art*	Textiles/fashion
Glasgow School of Art*	Design/textiles
Gloucestershire College of Art & Technology, Cheltenham	Fashion design

* In Scotland BA (Hons) courses last four years but the first year is regarded as an introductory course.

Goldsmiths College, School of Art & Design, London	Embroidery & textiles
Gray's School of Art, Robert Gordon's Institute of Technology, Aberdeen*	Textiles & surface decoration
Harrow College of Higher Education	Fashion/design
Huddersfield Polytechnic	Fashion design
Kingston Polytechnic	Fashion
Lancaster University	Art, design & marketing
Leicester Polytechnic	Fashion & textile design
Liverpool Polytechnic	Textiles & fashion design
Loughborough College of Art & Design	Textiles/fashion
Manchester Polytechnic	Textiles/fashion
Middlesex Polytechnic, Barnet	Textiles & fashion design
Newcastle upon Tyne Polytechnic	Fashion design & marketing
North East London Polytechnic	Fashion design & marketing
North Staffordshire Polytechnic	Design, multi-disciplinary
Nottingham Polytechnic	Fashion design
Polytechnic of Central London	Fashion
Ravensbourne College of Design & Communication, Bromley	Fashion
St Martins School of Art, London	Fashion/textiles
University of Leeds	Textile design
University of Ulster, Belfast	Textiles & fashion design
Winchester School of Art	Textiles design

BA (Hons) 4-year sandwich course

Brighton Polytechnic	Fashion/textiles design with administration
Kidderminster College of Further Education	Design of carpets & related textiles
Lancashire Polytechnic	Fashion
Newcastle upon Tyne Polytechnic	Fashion with marketing

North East London Polytechnic	Fashion/design with marketing
Trent Polytechnic, Nottingham	Knitwear design
St Martins School of Art, London	Fashion
Scottish College of Textiles, Galashiels	Textiles with clothing (also 5 years)
University of Ulster, Belfast	Textiles & fashion design

B.Sc. (Hons) 3 years full time

Bradford University	Clothing management/ technology
University of Leeds	Textile studies
University of Manchester Institute of Science & Technology	Textile design, and design management, Textile technology, textile economics & management

B.Sc. (Hons) 4 years full time

Huddersfield Polytechnic	Textile design (sandwich course)
University of Manchester, Institute of Science & Technology	Clothing engineering with integrated industrial training
Scottish College of Textiles, Galashiels	Textiles with clothing (also 5-year sandwich course)

Postgraduate Courses

Diploma 1 year full time

Central School of Art & Design	Textile design
Duncan of Jordanstone College of Art, Dundee	Printed textiles
Edinburgh College of Art	Fashion, theatre costume, woven textiles
Glasgow School of Art	Embroidery & woven textiles, printed textile design

Gray's School of Art, Robert Gordon's Institute of Technology, Aberdeen	Textile design
Leeds University	Textile design
Scottish College of Textiles, Galashiels	Textile design
University of Ulster, Belfast	Textile/fashion

MA 1 year full time

City of Birmingham Polytechnic	Textiles/fashion

MA 4 terms full time

Leicester Polytechnic	Fashion & textile design options in footwear & knitted fabric design
Manchester Polytechnic	Textiles/fashion
Nottingham Polytechnic	Knitwear & knitted fabric design

MA 5 Terms part time

St Martins School of Art, London	Textiles/fashion design

MA (RCA) or M.Des. (RCA) 2 years full time

Royal College of Art, London	Fashion design & textile design

M.Phil. 1 year full time

Huddersfield Polytechnic	Textile design

M.Phil. 1 year or 2 years full or part time

Winchester School of Art	Textiles/fashion research

13 Looking for Work

There are two main routes to finding work. The first is as a freelance designer, independently working from your own base on commissions for a variety of clients. This will involve taking your portfolio around to a number of potential clients and trying to sell your ideas and skills. This takes time and often the need to be supported by other forms of employment.

The second route is to find employment in manufacturing, retailing or marketing, as part of a production team working full time for one company or being a member of a consultancy to a number of companies. Work within fashion/textiles design is very competitive and the market is continually fluctuating. Most of the opportunities are to be found in the large towns and cities.

It is important to remember that employers are looking for a number of factors:

- Qualifications

- Portfolio

- The way you present yourself

- Are you enthusiastic?

- Are you co-operative, able to be part of a team?

- Are you adaptable, able to take the initiative?

- Are you able to work to deadline and various constraints?

- Are you in touch with the general world of art and design and particularly new developments in your specialist field?

There are three main ways of finding work:

1 Job advertisements
2 Approaching potential employers
3 Employing an agent

Job advertisements It is a must to read regularly the job sections in the newspapers, design journals and specialist professional journals, some of which are listed below:

Newspapers
Guardian (Creative and Media page, Mondays)
Independent (Creative and Media page, Wednesdays)
The Times (Media page, Wednesdays)

Weekly magazines
Drapers' Record
Fashion Weekly
Menswear
Design Week
Shoe and Leather News
The Times Educational Supplement
The Times Higher Educational Supplement } for teaching posts

Monthly magazines
Apparel International
Fashion Extra
Design

Approaching potential employers Approaching a potential employer, either looking for full-time work or as a freelance, will involve carefully researching the market, making a list of the target companies/people and writing letters of introduction. If they are interested they will make an appointment with you to look at your portfolio and see how you strike them as a person.

Another way of contacting employers is to go to an employment agency. Agencies will try to match you to a suitable vacancy on their files. They do not charge you a fee: the employer has to pay. All agencies will want a copy of your c.v. and some will want to see your portfolio.

Employment agency addresses:

> Atlas Fashion Division
> Third Floor
> 104 Baker Street
> London W1

Design Moves
The Chartered Society of Designers
29 Bedford Square
London WC1B 3EG

Menswear/Womenswear
207 Regent Street
London W1R 7DD

Price Jamieson & Partners Ltd
Paramount House
103/108 Oxford Street
London W1N 9FE

Employing an agent   An agent represents freelance designers and
is someone who will have many contacts in industry with potential
clients. Agents will try to sell your work to the best buyer rather than
get you a job.

The advantages are:

- It saves you time
- They have a range of clients, and clients contact them
- They are experienced in selling
- They will also negotiate contacts and chase payments

The disadvantages are:

- They will want twenty-five to forty per cent commission
- They are not keen on taking on people who are just
  beginning
- They like to have sole representation of your work
- You do not usually meet the client

Going Freelance

For those intending to become freelance or set up their own business,
there are many organizations and publications to help and advise.
Working for oneself can be a viable option but it needs very careful
thought before making the final decision.

- Would it be helpful to gain further experience by working for a design group or in industry or retailing first?

- Are you self-motivated and disciplined, able to work very much on your own, maybe for very long hours?

- Are you able to sell your ideas and skills?

- Do you have determination and a positive attitude to cope with setbacks and lack of security?

- Are you well organized with a business sense and good at managing many variables?

- Are you willing to risk borrowing the necessary capital or lay your own savings on the line?

- You must put in writing and ensure you have your client's agreement on what is commissioned, the time allocation and your fees, before starting any work.

- The copyright on the design belongs to you unless you assign it to your client in writing.

- You will need a good accountant to help you at the beginning with book-keeping and to prepare a cashflow projection for at least the first twelve months of operating.

The following organizations are useful if you are intending to set up your own business:

Small Firms Service

This is a government agency providing a free information service and low-cost consultancy service. For your centre dial 100 and ask for Freephone Enterprise.

Local Enterprise Agencies

These offer advice to small firms at a local level. They provide free information, counselling and contacts to help with starting up and running a small business. Details of your nearest agency may be obtained from:

Business in the Community
227A City Road
London EC1V 1SU
01 253 3716

The Welsh Development Agency
The South Wales Valley Office
Treforest
Pontypridd
Mid Glamorgan CF37 5UT
0443 841131

The Scottish Development Agency
Small Business Division
Roseberry House
Haymarket Terrace
Edinburgh EH12 5EZ
031 337 9595

The Local Enterprise Development Unit
Lamont House
Purdy's Lane
Newtonbreda
Belfast BT8 4AR
0232 691 031

The Rural Development Commission

This is a government service for small businesses in rural areas and country towns. It provides advice and low-cost consultancy. It also provides training, help in finding premises and a number of loan and grant schemes. The head office is:

The Rural Development Commission
141 Castle Street
Salisbury FP1 3TP
0722 336255

The Commission also has thirty area offices which are listed in the telephone directories.

Joining a Professional Body

Career development is often helped by membership of the appropriate professional body serving the specialist field. Obtaining membership varies. Sometimes it is granted after leaving college and having your work vetted by the membership board, sometimes it is only given after having worked for a minimum period of time.

Not only is it a granting of a professional qualification but it also gives you the opportunity to use certain facilities and services – such as the Designers' Register operated by the Chartered Society of Designers. This service has two functions. One: the Freelance Register which consists of files giving details of self-employed designers or design practices. Potential clients are sent copies or invited to see the register at the CSD's offices. Two: the Staff Vacancies Register, which contains details of its members looking for full-time or part-time jobs. Employers who notify the CSD of vacancies are sent photocopies of the forms of suitable candidates on the Register. Interviews are arranged by the employer. The CSD would also be able to recommend agencies/agents.

Going into Teaching

If, after you have completed your first degree, you wish to make a career teaching design in schools, you will need to do a further year's postgraduate training. This will either be a specialist art teachers' qualification, an ATC or ATD (Art Teacher's Certificate or Diploma), or a more general teaching qualification, the PGCE (Postgraduate Certificate of Education).

Further information, course addresses and application forms can be obtained from:

ATC/ATD
The Clearing House for Postgraduate courses in
Art and Design Education
Penn House
9 Broad Street
Hereford HR4 9AP

PGCE
Graduate Teacher Training Registry
3 Crawford Place
London W1H 2B

14 Things to Read, Useful Addresses and Trade Fairs

Things to read

Design magazines
Blueprint
Crafts
Design
Design Week

Fashion and accessory magazines
British Jeweller
Drapers' Record
Elle
Fashion Extra
Fashion Weekly
Menswear
Shoe and Leather News
Retail Jeweller
Vogue

Useful Addresses

Fibre Manufacturers and Organizations

Bayer
4 James Street
Bradford BD1 3PZ

Courtaulds
Henrietta House
9 Henrietta Place
London W1A 4SN

Enka
PO Box 62
Enkalon House
Regent Road
Leicester LE1 9AF

ICI
PR and Promotions Department
ICI Fibres
5th Floor, Bowater House
Knightsbridge
London SW1X 7LN

International Institute for Cotton
Fashion Department
21 Cavendish Place
London W1M 9DL

International Linens
31 Great Queen Street
London WC2 5BA

International Wool Secretariat
Fashion House
6 Carlton Gardens
London SW1Y 5AE

Clothing and Allied Industries Organizations

British Footwear Manufacturers' Federation
Royalty House
72 Dean Street
London W1V 5HB

British Hat Guild
Commerce House
Stuart Street
Luton LU1 5AU

British Jewellery and Giftwear Federation Ltd
27 Frederick Street
Birmingham B1 3HJ

British Knitting and Clothing Export Council
British Apparel Centre
7 Swallow Place
London W1R 7AA

British Leather Federation
Leather Trade House
Kings Park Road
Moulton Park
Northampton NN3 1JD

British Man-made Fibres Federation
24 Buckingham Gate
London SW1E 6LB

British Standards Institution
Park Street
London W1A 2BS

British Textile Confederation
24 Buckingham Gate
London SW1E 6LB

Clothing and Footwear Institute
71 Brushfield Street
London E1 6AA

Glove Guild of Great Britain
Shell House
138 Plumstead Common Road
London SE18 2VL

National Association of Glove Manufacturers
Crane and Partners
20–21 Tooks Court
Cursitor Street
London EC4A 1LB

Scottish Woollen Publicity Council
45 Moray Place
Edinburgh EH3 6EQ

Worshipful Company of Goldsmiths
Goldsmiths' Hall
Foster Lane
London EC2V 6BN

British Apparel Centre
7 Swallow Street
London W1R 7AA

British Hand Knitting Association Ltd
Park House
57–59 Well Street
Bradford BD1 5NQ

Clothing and Allied Products Industry Training Board
80 Richardshaw Lane
Pudsey
Leeds LS28 6BN

Textile Institute
10 Blackfriars Street
Manchester M3 5DR

Scottish Woollen Industries
45 Moray Place
Edinburgh EH3 6EQ

Design Organizations

Chartered Society of Designers
29 Bedford Square
London WC1B 3EG

Crafts Council
1 Oxendon Street
London SW1Y 4AT

The Design Council
28 Haymarket
London SW1Y 4SU

Design Council, Northern Ireland
Windsor House
9–15 Bedford Street
Belfast BT2 7EG

Design Council, Scotland
72 St Vincent Street
Glasgow G2 5TN

Y Cyngor Cynllunio
Design Council, Wales
Pearl Assurance House
Greyfriars Road
Cardiff CF1 3JN

Society of Designer Craftsmen
24 Rivington Street
London EC2

Business Information

City Business Library
Gillett House
55 Basinghall Street
London EC2

Craft Point
Beauly
Inverness-shire IV4 7EH

The Department of Trade and Industry headquarters
The Enterprise Initiative
British Overseas Trade Board
1 Victoria Street
London SW1H 0ET

Department of Trade and Industry
Business Statistics Office
Government Buildings
Cardiff Road
Newport
Gwent NP9 1XG

Department of Trade and Industry
Small Firms Information Centre
8–10 Bulstrode Street
London W1M 7FT

Economic Development Committee for the Distributive Trades
NEDO (National Economics Development Office)
Millbank Tower
21 Millbank
London SW1P 4QX

Economist Intelligence Unit
Spencer House
27 St James's Place
London W1A 1BW

Export Buying Offices Association (EXPO)
c/o Portman Ltd
360 Oxford Street
London W1A 4BX

Science Reference Library (Holborn)
25 Southampton Buildings
Chancery Lane
London WC2

Scottish Development Agency
Roseberry House
Haymarket Terrace
Edinburgh EH12 5EZ

Clothing and Footwear Journal
The Old School
Station Road
Northampton NN7 1LT

Museums with Major Fashion Collections

Museum of Costume
Assembly Rooms
Bath BA1 2QH

Museum of Costume
King's Park
Glasgow G44 5HL

Victoria and Albert Museum
South Kensington
London SW7 2RL

Gallery of English Costume
Platt Fields
Rusholme
Manchester M14 5LL

In addition to these major exhibitions many museums have interesting collections. Some, as in the case of the shoe collection in the Northampton Museum and Art Gallery, relate to local industries. Some manufacturers have museums open to the public – the Clark's shoe collection at Street in Somerset being particularly remarkable.

Trade Fairs in Britain

THE LONDON SHOW   Mid-season womenswear
London: February and September

LONDON PRET A PORTER   Womenswear
London: February

IMBEX   Menswear
London: February

BRITISH YARN SHOW
Leicester: February and September

LEATHER & ASSOCIATED TRADE FAIR
London: March

BRITISH DESIGNER SHOW/THE LONDON COLLECTIONS
Womenswear
London: March and October

BRITISH FOOTWEAR FAIR   Footwear
Birmingham: March

FABREX   Fabrics
London: March and September

MAB   Menswear
London: August

TEXPRINT   Textile designs
London: September

BRITISH FOOTWEAR FAIR   Footwear
London: October